ADVANCING CORE COMPETENCIES
Emphasizing Practice Behaviors and Outcomes

QUIENTON NICHOLS
Kennesaw State University

PEARSON

Boston   Columbus   Indianapolis   New York   San Francisco   Upper Saddle River
Amsterdam   Cape Town   Dubai   London   Madrid   Milan   Munich   Paris   Montreal   Toronto
Delhi   Mexico City   Sao Paulo   Sydney   Hong Kong   Seoul   Singapore   Taipei   Tokyo

Editorial Director: Craig Campanella
Editor in Chief: Dickson Musslewhite
Executive Editor: Ashley Dodge
Editorial Product Manager: Carly Czech
**Vice-President, Director of
    Marketing:** Brandy Dawson
Executive Marketing Manager: Jeanette Koskinas
Senior Marketing Manager: Wendy Albert
Marketing Assistant: Jessica Warren
Media Editor: Felicia Halpert
Managing Editor: Melissa Feimer

Senior Production Project Manager/Liaison:
    Barbara Cappuccio
Senior Operations Specialist: Brian Mackey
Art Director, Cover: Jayne Conte
Cover Designer: Karen Salzbach
Full-Service Project Management: Hemalatha,
    Integra Software Services, Pvt. Ltd.
Composition: Integra Software Services, Pvt. Ltd.
Printer/Binder: Edwards Brothers
Cover Printer: Lehigh-Phoenix Color/
    Hagerstown

Library of Congress Cataloging-in-Publication Data
Nichols, Quienton.
    Advancing core competencies : emphasizing practice behaviors and outcomes/Quienton Nichols.—1st ed.
        p. cm.
    Includes bibliographical references.
    ISBN-13: 978-0-205-20228-7
    ISBN-10: 0-205-20228-4
    1. Social service.   2. Social work education.   3. Evidence-based social work.   4. Core competencies.
    5. Professional ethics.   I. Title.
    HV40.N525 2012
    361.3—dc23

                                                                                2011028472

10 9 8 7 6 5 4 3 2 1

ISBN-10: 0-205-20228-4
ISBN-13: 978-0-205-20228-7

CONTENTS

1

PROFESSIONAL IDENTITY

CSWE EPAS 2.1.1 *Identify as a professional social worker and conduct oneself accordingly*

Professional identity is the first core competency of the 2008 Educational Policy and Accreditation Standards (EPAS) and provides a solid basis for understanding for the advanced or second year social work student. As an advanced or second year student practitioner, you will continue to develop your understanding of the multiplicity of roles and identities of social workers. You will learn that social workers serve as representatives of the profession, particularly in their support of the profession's mission and the adoption of its core values. You will be taught the intricate steps by which social workers commit themselves to the profession's enhancement, as well as to their own professional behavior and development. In your advanced or second year course loads, your professional identity will be enhanced as you learn more of social work's rich history which goes beyond Jane Addams and Hull House. In your perspective MSW programs, you will shape your professional identity as you learn of social work icons such as Bertha Capen Reynolds, Richard Cabot, Whitney M. Young, Jr., and Dorcas Bowles.

You will also learn that securing an understanding of the operational practice behaviors of the professional identity of social workers will enhance your practicum experience in the field at your perspective internships. As an advanced social work student, you will learn to advocate for client access to the services of social work. You will identify with a myriad of roles and responsibilities during your advanced year as you reflect on the different services and programs that you were introduced to during your foundation year. You will also learn how to practice personal reflection and self-correction in an effort to ensure continual professional development; and the importance of attending to professional roles and maintaining appropriate boundaries as you demonstrate professional demeanor in behavior, appearance, and communication. As an advanced or second year social work student, you will gain knowledge of the importance of engaging in career-long learning and the value of supervision and consultation in your perspective practices. Learning to identify yourself as a professional social worker in both conduct and demeanor will connect your academic knowledge with practical application as you bridge the knowledge, values, and skills of social work with the operational practice behaviors of the profession.

ADVOCATING FOR CLIENT ACCESS TO SOCIAL WORK SERVICES

In your advanced or second year, you will learn the necessity for advocating for client access to any and all eligible and entitled social work services that they may receive. You will learn that supporting or advocating for clients' rights for services is more than just providing a list of needed services such as food stamps, unemployment benefits, or Supplemental Security Income (SSI). It is more than educating the client about agencies such as the Department of Family and Children Services, the Labor Department, or the Social Security Administration. As an advanced or second year MSW student, you will discover that the profession of social work offers a delivery system of services that provide assistance relative to the personal and/or social problems of the client. You will learn that social work services are inclusive of a wide range of agencies and programs such as: social service agencies; private agencies; hospitals and clinics; mental health centers; and advocacy programs.

The field of social work is known by many as "the major profession that delivers social services in governmental and private organizations throughout the world." The profession seeks to empower people and to identify and build on the strengths that exist in them and in their communities. As you learn to advocate for the client, you will assist them in preventing future problems or resolving existing problems in psychosocial functioning and/ or in achieving life-enhancing goals, with an ultimate goal of creating a just society. As an advanced or second year MSW student, you will learn the importance of the affiliations and orientations within a private practice milieu; social service departments; community mental health centers; hospitals and clinics; counseling centers and churches; private nonprofit groups and citizen groups; and as social change activists. As you learn how to advocate for client access to social work services, you will develop a basic understanding of the uniqueness of the social work profession and its goal of social justice for all.

PERSONAL REFLECTION AND SELF-CORRECTION

Boundaries serve many purposes that support personal reflection, self-correction, and provide an avenue of protection when situations arise where one may feel that someone is behaving in inappropriate or unacceptable way.

You will begin to recognize the importance of the therapeutic relationship, and the person-in-environment and strengths perspectives, and these will guide your personal reflection and self-correction. Your personal reflections and self-corrections are rooted in understanding your attributes and increasing your self-awareness. You will learn that developing a keen insight into precisely what you do best and what you need to learn more about will expand your personal reflection and assist in accurately assessing your need for professional self-correction. Although the same values and attitudes are basic to social work, there are, for example, differences between the kinds of people who can do intensive, one-to-one therapy and those who fare best in the rough grassroots atmosphere of community advocacy. Self-awareness can be seen as a way to remove inner roadblocks or challenges that might otherwise professionally impede your progress; however, self-awareness allows you to confront your challenges and work toward finding solutions to them. You will learn that self-awareness is vital for all professions but is an indispensable quality for social workers. Some of the many personal characteristics of self-awareness include: attitude toward change, family roots, lifestyle, manner in which you meet personal needs, moral codes, the personal biases and stereotypes we embrace, responses to various life circumstances, and values (Johnson & Yanca, 2010).

You will learn that having knowledge of your personal ideologies enhances the process of self-correction. Knowledge of the way in which you feel about a situation is particularly important in case there is a need for self-correction. Just as no two people are alike, no two people's backgrounds are identical. Each of you comes to the social work profession with unique sets of philosophies. For example, you might draw from your spiritual upbringing or moral codes, while others might draw from their general ethical framework. You will learn that more often than not your values will come under scrutiny by your cohorts in the classroom, by your supervisor at your internship site, and possibly by your clients at your practicum agencies. However, there are a plethora of steps in the self-correction process; the first couple of steps are (1) identifying the issues of concern to reflect upon by documenting behavioral patterns as they come to mind; and (2) acknowledging the problem openly while looking for a solution.

You may find that for some it is important to state your feelings out loud and to precede the feeling with "I feel" while in the self-correcting process. Emotions do not define you—they are a form of internal communication that help you understand yourself. To some, setting boundaries can be seen as a more refined technique of manipulation. For example, you might operate with the belief that you are setting boundaries for your client, when in fact, you are attempting to manipulate. The difference, you will learn, in setting healthy boundaries and manipulating is that when setting boundaries, you release yourself of the outcome.

PROFESSIONAL ROLES AND BOUNDARIES

Your professional roles and boundaries will become clearer during your advanced or second year in your perspective MSW programs as you are better able to learn of past icons in the professions. According to Suppes and Wells (2009), professional roles are defined as the behaviors expected from persons, through education and legal certification, to provide services in a specific profession. For social workers, role expectations are often not clearly understood by the general public, so it becomes very important that you know of the profession's rich history when trying to define your role. You learned of Jane Addams and Mary Richmond during your foundation year. Jane Addams could easily be seen in the role of initiator, as she called attention to problems or to potential problems and was a founder of the U. S. Settlement House Movement. She was also the second woman to be awarded the Nobel Peace Prize and obtained worldwide recognition in the first third of the twentieth century as a pioneer social worker. During that era, Jane Addams was the country's most prominent woman, through her writing, settlement work, and international efforts for world peace. Mary Richmond could be seen in the case manager role and was one of the founders of the social work profession. In 1917, she published the book *Social Diagnosis,* which defined the casework process to as include: information gathering, diagnosis, prognosis, and treatment planning.

You will also learn that much of the professional identity of social work was shaped by earlier social workers like Bertha Capen Reynolds, Richard Cabot, and Harriett Bartlett and that their roles help clarify and validate your roles, even today. Bertha Capen Reynolds was a social advocate for working-class and oppressed groups who opposed the medical model but focused on clients' strengths. She emphasized the importance of social workers' support for social justice and civil rights through political activities. Richard Cabot introduced medical social work at Massachusetts General Hospital in Boston and was a broker of medical services for many impoverished clients in the Boston area. Harriett Bartlett was a practitioner who conceptualized generalist social work practice and saw the central focus of social work as helping people cope with life situations and balance the demands of their social environments. She felt that social work should reflect concerns for individuals in the context of their situations (DuBois & Miley, 2011).

During your advanced or second year, your professional identity will be further shaped as you learn and study great minds like Whitney M. Young, Jr. and Robert Hill. Whitney M. Young, Jr. can be seen in the role of an activist. You will learn that an activist seeks basic institutional change in which the objective often involves a shift in power and resources to a disadvantaged group. Whitney M. Young, Jr. was an American civil rights leader who served as executive director of the National Urban League, an organization that fought for equitable access to socioeconomic opportunity for the historically disenfranchised. He served as dean of the School of Social Work at Atlanta University (now Clark

Atlanta University) from 1954 to 1960. The School of Social Work at Clark Atlanta was renamed the Whitney M. Young, Jr. School of Social Work in his honor. Robert Hill can be seen in the role of coordinator because he was instrumental in bringing components together in an organized manner when he identified the strengths of black families in his book *Strengths of Black Families.*

You will become confident in your professional identity as you learn of great social work educators such as Leon Chestang, Florence Hollis, and Dorcas Bowles. Leon Chestang was a graduate of the University of Chicago who later became dean of the School of Social Work at Wayne State University. Several of Dr. Chestang's articles focused on character development in a hostile environment, in which he described how the sense of "two-ness" is experienced by black people who often must live in two worlds—the majority world, and the minority world of their ethnic background. Florence Hollis did pioneering work in social work education. In 1939, she wrote *Social Casework for Practice: Six Case Studies,* which was used by social work educators throughout the United States. Her last book, *Casework: A Psychosocial Therapy,* was outstanding for understanding social work theory and practice. She taught at Columbia University School of Social Work for twenty-five years. Dr. Dorcas Bowles was an educator who was instrumental in infusing diversity and cultural competency in social work education. She coined the term *ethnic sense of self,* which demonstrated how the "sense of self" for the black child is developed.

You will also further your understanding of boundaries as articulated through the NASW Code of Ethics. You will learn about the importance of professional boundaries with clients, cohorts, and colleagues. Boundaries can be seen as the ability to know where you end and where another person begins and includes concepts such as space, setting limits, determining acceptable behavior, and creating a sense of autonomy. When you learn where you end and others begin you can then closely engage with others because you seldom feel overwhelmed or unprotected. You will learn that having a sense of autonomy prevents the need to distance yourself from others with a barrier. Professional boundaries are important because they define the limits and responsibilities of the people with whom you will interact within the profession. When professional boundaries are clearly defined you will become more efficient and confident of your professional identity.

PROFESSIONAL DEMEANOR IN BEHAVIOR, APPEARANCE, AND COMMUNICATION

Your professional demeanor in behavior, appearance, and communication will add to your professional identity. You will learn that your professional demeanor is more than your professional title, the way in which you respond to others, or even your assumed roles. It is seldom defined in terms of a job description, but can be clearly outlined within interpersonal characteristics that are unique to each individual. You will learn that professional boundaries have a direct relationship to interpersonal characteristics, in that professional boundaries substantially impact your professional behavior, appearance, and communication regarding your workplace performance, and the quality of the social environment. Interpersonal-characteristic parameters could include: (1) the tone people use with each other; (2) the attitude and approach co-workers use with each other; (3) the ability to focus on work objectives even with people you do not like or with whom you are having personal conflict; (4) the ability to effectively set limits with others who have poor boundaries; and (5) clearly defining the consequences when a boundary is violated and sticking to it (Sabey & Gafner, 1996).

You will learn that there are many core skill areas that you can adopt that will aid you in managing professional boundaries, three of which are:

(1) knowing your limits: what you can do well within the allotted time frame;
(2) tactfully and openly communicating about goals and limitations; and
(3) being available to discuss differences and reach agreements.

Knowing your limits, such as what you can do well within the allotted time frame, is very important when establishing boundaries. In your foundation internships, you possibly witnessed professionals exaggerating their aptitudes and overselling their capabilities and possibly not providing accurate estimates of what they can or cannot do. During your advanced or second year, you will learn not to exaggerate your abilities by overselling them but that you must give accurate estimates of what you can do. Providing good-quality service in a timely manner will improve your credibility, while missing deadlines or delivering a substandard product will only hurt your reputation.

Tactfully and openly communicating about goals and limitations will also help build your professional boundaries. You will learn that denigrating or misrepresenting your abilities will artificially prevent you from being able to demonstrate your professional skills, which might affect service delivery and your career advancement. When discussing your limitations, focus on what you want and what you are willing to do to get it. Keep your focus on your positive intentions; ask for help when it's needed to ensure good-quality work; actively engage in problem solving; and do not complain about the problem, yet make all attempts to ensure that others are receiving the message you intended by asking for feedback when it's not forthcoming. Lastly, you will learn that you must be available to discuss differences and reach agreements. Reflect back your understanding of the other person's needs, interests, and concerns. Attempt to negotiate win–win solutions. Establishing professional roles and boundaries goes hand-in-hand with managing interpersonal relationships within the profession and establishing professional, productive environments based on trust.

ENGAGING IN CAREER-LONG LEARNING

You will discover that continuing career-long learning, beyond your MSW degree, is important if you want to stay on the cutting edge of knowledge regarding the practices of social work. The core concept of career-long learning is that you learn from cradle (receipt of your MSW degree) to grave (the retirement years) and that individual progress occurs from one learning level to the next throughout your professional lifetime. Each learning event is a continuous progression to the next learning event and is never isolated or a means to an end. You will learn that there are many ways by which to continue career-long learning: (1) in-service training; (2) fulfillment of state licensing requirements; (3) Continuing Education Units (CEUs) and academic credits; (4) distance-education courses; and (5) preparation for additional professional degrees. You will learn that policies to encourage career-long learning are based on the view that you must obtain new knowledge primarily to secure and to maintain employment in an ever-changing world.

In-service training within your agency setting is another step to continuing your quest for knowledge as a career-long learner. Often these trainings are facilitated by experts in the particular topic area, who are outside of the agency. Another way to continue the cycle of learning as a postgraduate is through the fulfillment of state licensing requirements for professional titles and designations such as Licensed Master Social Worker (LMSW), Licensed Social Worker (LSW), Licensed Clinical Social Worker (LCSW), or the Academy of Certified Social Workers (ACSW). Yet another method to career-long learning is by attending meetings or trainings that offer CEUs. There is an array of approaches to obtaining CEUs. You can secure CEUs at conferences such as the Council on Social Work Education Annual Program Meeting (CSWE APM), which is held annually at various U. S. locations. You can also continue the cycles of your learning via distance education and furthering your graduate studies through your pursuit of various doctoral degrees.

USING SUPERVISION AND CONSULTATION

You will continue to see the importance of supervision and consultation in managing your professional career at the postgraduate level. Supervision and consultation are vital personal links in service delivery at your agency—paid or voluntary. They constitute the interactive process through which the agency's mission, goals, and values are communicated and interpreted concerning your professional roles, professional demeanor, goals, and interpersonal characteristics. You will learn that supervision and consultation are key not only to your success, but to the success of your agency or organization. By utilizing supervision and consultation, you will learn and understand your responsibilities; improve your work performance, and better organize your resources to assist your client base.

Mark Smith (2005) explained Alfred Kadushin's approach to the function of supervision in social work in terms of (1) administrative, (2) educational, and (3) supportive models. The administrative model of supervision involves the support and continuance of "superior principles of work, coordination of practice with policies of administration, the assurance of an efficient and smooth-running office" (Smith, 2005). The educational model is concerned with the educational development of individuals to the point that they fully realize their possibilities of usefulness, while the supportive model of supervision is the maintenance of harmonious working relationships within the agency (Smith, 2005). In administrative supervision, the primary problem is concerned with the correct, effective, and appropriate implementation of agency policies and procedures, with a primary goal of ensuring adherence to policy and procedure. While educational supervision is concerned with workers' ignorance and/or ineptitude regarding the knowledge, attitude, and skills required to do the job, supportive supervision's primary goal is to improve morale and job satisfaction (Smith, 2005).

PRACTICE PROFESSIONAL BEHAVIORS AND ASSESS OUTCOMES

This section will help further your understanding of the practice behaviors to the 2008 CSWE EPAS 2.1.1. *Identify as a professional social worker and conduct oneself accordingly:* (1) advocate for client access to the services of social work; (2) practice personal reflection and self-correction to assure continual professional development; (3) attend to professional roles and boundaries; (4) demonstrate professional demeanor in behavior, appearance, and communication; (5) engage in career-long learning; and (6) use supervision and consultation. Each question that follows will test your application of the practice behaviors and your ability to think critically regarding their function. The questions are deliberately varied and randomly placed regarding the six professional identity practice behaviors.

Multiple Choice

(Note: On the lines below each multiple-choice question, explain why you chose that particular answer.)

Difficulty Scale: ✳ = Easy   ✳ ✳ = Moderate   ✳ ✳ ✳ = Challenging

1. You are in your final semester of your advanced or concentration year, interning at an AIDS service organization (ASO). Jane is a new client at the ASO assigned to your case load and has recently learned that she is HIV positive. Jane is adamant that she will not tell anyone that she is seeking psychological services from the ASO and, in fact, intends to continue having sex with her boyfriend, Jack. While proving professional services, you learn that Jane's boyfriend, Jack, is a distant relative of yours. What should you do as her social worker?

    a. Break the confidentiality and inform Jack that Jane is a client where you work but not provide him the name of the ASO.
    b. Continue to see Jane and encourage her to tell her boyfriend, Jack, about her HIV status.
    c. Refer Jane to a doctor who specializes in HIV-positive clients.
    d. Terminate your client relationship with Jane.

    Difficulty: ✳ ✳ = Moderate
    Topic: Professional boundaries
    Practice Behavior: Attend to professional roles and boundaries

    _____

    _____

2. While interning at an AIDS service organization (ASO), you learn that Frank's condition is worsening and he requires around-the-clock care; however, he was refused admittance to We Care, a nursing home close to his residence. What should you, the social worker, do initially?

    a. Mediate with the nursing home, We Care.
    b. Obtain a lawyer on Frank's behalf.
    c. Advocate for Frank in an effort to make We Care accept him as a patient.
    d. Arrange for home care for Frank.

    Difficulty: ✳ = Easy
    Topic: Social worker as an advocate
    Practice Behavior: Advocate for client access to the services of social work

    _____

    _____

3. You are interning at an agency that provides in-house supportive services for the elderly, and your client Zelda has recently lost her husband of forty-two years and is now living alone. She has been receiving home health aide services for two weeks but has lately been complaining that she believes that the service providers are stealing from her. You should consider which of the following?

   a. Zelda is trying to manipulate your agency to get her way.
   b. Zelda is having difficulty adjusting to the dependent role, and the services that are being provided for her are appropriate services.
   c. Zelda needs to be placed in a nursing home.
   d. Zelda is in need of a new aide.

   Difficulty: ✲✲ = Moderate
   Topic: Social work services
   Practice Behavior: Advocate for client access to the services of social work

   _____

   _____

4. You have recently been hired for the staff of a relatively new agency at which policy development regarding service delivery to clients is a priority. You can best inform your supervisor about the effects of policy on clients by:

   a. Discussing policy with other staff and feeding back complaints to supervisor.
   b. Letting your supervisor know all of the policy's faults.
   c. Letting your supervisor know how policy affects clients.
   d. Writing a memo to the director.

   Difficulty: ✲ = Easy
   Topic: Professional identity
   Practice Behavior: Using supervision and consultation

   _____

   _____

5. At your celebratory MSW graduation party, your next-door neighbor reveals to you that he feels guilty about recently having sex with his fifteen-year-old daughter. What is your best course of action?

   a. Give him the names and phone numbers of counselors, because he had been drinking at the party and might not be aware of what he is saying.
   b. Remain quiet and do nothing, because he knows where you live.
   c. Report him to protective services.

d. Tell him to stop this behavior with his daughter and stress to him what could happen if he does not stop.

Difficulty: ✳ = Easy
Topic: Professional identity
Practice Behavior: Advocate for client access to the services of social work

_____

_____

6. Your second cousin Junior Smith is court ordered to receive anger management because of his violent temper and hatred toward women. You know that your internship agency is on the list of court-approved providers, so you refer him to your agency but let your supervisor, Frances, know that Junior is a relative. During a family outing, Junior shares with you that he plans to rape and murder the supervisor, Frances, after a session because "She has it coming to her." As a social worker, what is your best approach?

   a. Allow Junior to ventilate and tell him that he had better not mess up his chances of employment after graduating with this agency.
   b. Discuss alternatives to violence with Junior.
   c. Tell the supervisor and the police of Junior's plans.
   d. Consult with the agency's psychiatrist and suggest that Junior receive medication.

Difficulty: ✳ ✳ = Moderate
Topic: Professional boundaries
Practice Behavior: Attend to professional roles and boundaries

_____

_____

7. You are a Licensed Master Social Worker (LMSW) at Helping Hands, a local nonprofit agency that specializes in geriatric services. Mary, a sixty-three-year-old female, has recently suffered from a stroke and is slightly confused and disoriented; however, she does recognize members of her family. Because of her stroke and mental state, one of the staff psychiatrists at Helping Hands recommends that Mary participate in rehabilitative services at a nearby nursing-home facility rather than at home with her daughter Martha. Martha objects and wants to continue to take care of her mother at home and says that with the help of her siblings, round-the-clock services can be provided for their mother. The first thing that you, Mary's social worker, should do is to:

   a. Send the client home with her daughter Martha.
   b. Have a family meeting to discuss the recommendations.

    c. Refer the daughter to the doctor.

    d. Invite the daughter for a tour of the facility.

Difficulty: ✻ ✻ ✻ = Challenging

Topic: Social worker as an advocate

Practice Behavior: Advocate for client access to the services of social work

_____

_____

8. After several months of trying to take care of her mother, Susan and her siblings realize that, perhaps it was too much for them to do and that their mother, Alice, is having difficulty adjusting to living alone and caring for herself. What is the first action that you, her social worker, take?

    a. Go to the psychiatrist for a referral and secure a list of nursing homes where Alice might be able to reside.

    b. Apologize to the staff psychiatrist for questioning his authority.

    c. Arrange for supportive services for Alice and suggest that her children call and visit her as frequently as possible.

    d. Text a list of possible nursing homes to Susan and Alice.

Difficulty: ✻ ✻ = Moderate

Topic: Social work services

Practice Behavior: Advocate for client access to the services of social work

_____

_____

9. In your personal reflection time, you have noticed that during the weekly staffing of clients with all of the professionals, you sometimes feel apprehensive and very uncomfortable and limit your input regarding your clients. Particular anxiety is toward the psychiatrist at Helping Hands, because you feel that he is very knowledgeable of the use of psychotropic drugs and their effects on the clients. To better your understanding and participate more in the staff meetings, you should first:

    a. Speak with your supervisor and share your apprehensions and why you seldom add input in the staffings.

    b. Share with your supervisor your concerns and request possible workshops or in-service training that you can engage in to further your understanding of psychotropic drugs.

    c. Speak with the psychiatrist and ask him to suggest a book that you can read to better your understanding of how to participate in weekly staffings of clients.

d. Invite the psychiatrist to lunch and ask him about his educational background.

Difficulty: ✡✡✡ = Challenging
Topic: Engaging in career-long learning
Practice Behavior: Advocate for client access to the services of social work

____

____

10. You are a recent MSW graduate employed at the local Community Services Board (CSB). Your client requires a treatment method that you have no training for and were never taught in your MSW program. You, the social worker, should:

a. Study the literature about the treatment method and try to give the treatment.
b. Request that a social worker at another CSB, who is well trained in the method that your client is requesting, work with you.
c. Acknowledge that you are not familiar with the treatment and then speak with your supervisor and request that you refer the client to another counselor within your agency who is familiar with the treatment method requested by your client.
d. Use a treatment method that you are familiar with and disregard the client's request, and later Google the treatment method.

Difficulty: ✡✡ = Moderate
Topic: Practicing self-correction
Practice Behavior: Practice personal reflection and self-correction to ensure continual professional development

____

____

11. Suzanne is a client at the agency where you work as in independent contractor. She calls you to complain about her therapy with another social worker, James. She is very upset about a raise in the fee. You have recently shared your concerns with James regarding the high cost of his fees. You, the social worker, should:

a. Agree with Suzanne and then call James and give him your opinion.
b. Tell Suzanne that sliding fee scales are a requirement.
c. Tell Suzanne to speak directly with James about her concerns.

d. Refer her to a county agency with lower fees.

Difficulty: ✡ = Easy
Topic: Professional demeanor in behavior
Practice Behavior: Demonstrate professional demeanor in behavior, appearance, and communication

_____

_____

12. You are a supervisor at ABC Intervention Services. You have observed that Cynthia, an online staff member, habitually comes to work late, which subsequently delays the other crisis intervention specialist from leaving work on time. You, her supervisor, would most likely take which of the following actions?

   a. Discuss Cynthia's lateness with her immediately.
   b. Bring her lateness up for discussion at the staff meeting.
   c. Report Cynthia to the administration.
   d. Wait until Cynthia's performance appraisal to discuss her lateness.

Difficulty: ✡ = Easy
Topic: Supervision
Practice Behavior: Use of supervision and consultation

_____

_____

13. This is your first day interning at Best Love, and while conducting a session with a young couple, you discover that the girlfriend, Jane, refuses to continue having sexual intercourse with her boyfriend, Joe. You are aware that talking about controversial issues such as sexual intercourse between two unmarried people makes you very uncomfortable and judgmental. You, the social work intern, should:

   a. Refer them to Jeffrey, a seasoned sex therapist.
   b. Explore the sexual issues with the couple.
   c. Reassure them that their problems are not unusual.
   d. Refer them to an MD for physical exams.

Difficulty: ✡ ✡ ✡ = Challenging
Topic: Professional boundaries
Practice Behavior: Demonstrate professional demeanor in behavior, appearance, and communication

_____

_____

14. Tommy, your agency supervisor, is very comfortable with your ability to separate your personal views from your professional obligations and explains that he will conduct live supervision with you regarding the couple with sexual problems. As an MSW intern student, you understand "live supervision" to mean that Tommy:

    a. serves as a co-therapist to model clinical skills.
    b. is available to give feedback during the session.
    c. views the therapy session through Skype method while in another state.
    d. views videotapes of the supervisee in therapy and then offers feedback about the supervisee's clinical work.

    Difficulty: ✸✸✸ = Challenging
    Topic: Supervision
    Practice Behavior: Using supervision and consultation

    _____

    _____

15. You and an MSW cohort, Sarah, are receiving group supervision hours from Jeffrey of Best Love agency. You all have been working toward your licensure hours for over eighteen months and have further developed your professional relationship. You observe Sarah's behavior as being different and her appearance out of the norm. As the supervision continues, you determine that Sarah displays several prominent signs of depression. Which of the following should you do first?

    a. Obtain detailed information about Sarah's social history.
    b. Refer Sarah for psychological testing.
    c. Express your observation to Sarah and share with her that you are available to talk with her if she chooses.
    d. Investigate Sarah's support system.

    Difficulty: ✸✸✸ = Challenging
    Topic: Professional boundaries
    Practice Behavior: Attend to professional roles and boundaries

    _____

    _____

16. You are facilitating a group on sexual addictions at Best Love agency, and a man in the group admits to sexually molesting his two-year-old stepdaughter. He rationalizes by saying that he just could not resist her. You are outraged by his nonchalant behavior, but as a social worker, you should first:

    a. Approach the man after the group and tell him how inappropriate he was.

b. Stop the group meeting and call Child Protective Services (CPS).

c. Confront the man in the group session and ask him not to share that type of information.

d. Bring it to the attention of the group and let them respond to the man's comment while maintaining your professionalism.

Difficulty: ✵✵ = Moderate

Topic: Professional behavior

Practice Behavior: Demonstrate professional demeanor in behavior, appearance, and communication

---

17. Jeffrey's wife, Paula, has asked you to come over for dinner. Paula begins to tell you that her husband, Jeffrey, is physically abusive to her and that they separated two weeks ago. She further explained that her husband respects and likes you. Paula wants you, the social worker, to encourage Jeffrey to return home. You, the social worker, should:

a. Explain to Paula that it would be an inappropriate role for you as a social worker to take on.

b. Ask Jeffrey the next time you see him if he has considered marriage counseling.

c. Talk with Jeffrey separately about the importance of marriage.

d. Never mention your conversation with Paula and deny that you discussed the marriage with her.

Difficulty: ✵✵✵ = Challenging

Topic: Professional demeanor and professional roles and boundaries

Practice Behavior: Professional roles and boundaries

---

18. While a student in your MSW program, you learned that your sister Elizabeth is suffering from a chronic mental illness. You have been able to locate a great therapist for her to seek counseling from. However, Elizabeth tells you that she plans to kill the "mean old witch." In the past, Elizabeth has referred to her mother as the "mean old witch." What do you do first?

a. Nothing, as it is probably delusional thinking.

b. Refer Elizabeth to a psychiatrist.

c. Call the police.

d. Call your mother and tell her about Elizabeth's statement.

Difficulty: ✵✵ = Moderate
Topic: Professional behavior
Practice Behavior: Demonstrate professional demeanor in behavior, appearance, and communication

_____

_____

19. You are a social work student interning at Pulse Rehab. During a therapeutic group session that you facilitate, TJ, a group member, gives what he thinks is practical advice to the group. However, as TJ gives the advice, it is obvious to most of the group members that you are extremely agitated and annoyed. Subsequently, all the other members become very upset with TJ. As a social worker/group leader, you should:

   a. Encourage the group to move on and then schedule a session with TJ alone to give him constructive feedback about what he did.
   b. Respond actively by identifying what TJ did well and then offer constructive feedback.
   c. Ask each member of the group, including TJ, to point out what TJ did right and what he did wrong.
   d. Ask each member of the group, including TJ, to describe how he or she felt about what happened.

Difficulty: ✵✵✵ = Challenging
Topic: Self-correction
Practice Behavior: Practice personal reflection and self-correction to ensure continual professional development

_____

_____

20. You have recently graduated with your MSW and are now employed by Dells Counseling Agency (DCA), a wraparound provider that offers counseling services for the local courts in your county. You are asked to provide services to Marvin, who is mandated by the court to receive counseling. As Marvin is self-disclosing during the session, you remember hearing about a man who fell victim to identity theft and was falsely arrested for an offense that he did not commit. In spite of your best efforts to encourage Marvin to follow the court order and allow justice to take its course, he calmly states that he does not need nor does he want to be in counseling and shares with you that he is not planning to continue with counseling. You then began to believe that the courts made a mistake and that Marvin was truly an innocent man.

_____

Subsequently, Marvin fails to show up for the second session. You, the social worker, should:

a. Report the outcome of therapy to the court and share your professional findings.
b. Contact the client and ask him why he does not want to come back to therapy.
c. Contact the client and explain the court order.
d. Maintain the client's confidentiality and respect his decision.

Difficulty: ✵ ✵ = Moderate
Topic: Advocate for the client
Practice Behavior: Advocate for client access to the services of social work

_____

_____

21. You are about to graduate with your MSW and are interested in becoming a wraparound provider for your county and provide counseling services to clients of the court system. You already have some knowledge of what wraparound services provide because you interned with Dells Counseling Agency (DCA). The best and most productive method by which to become a wraparound provider is to:

a. Google "How to become a wraparound provider in your state."
b. Contact the owner of DCA and share with him your desire and/or plans to become a provider within your county.
c. Contact your immediate supervisor at DCA and ask her about becoming a wraparound provider.
d. Attend a two-day seminar on how to become a wraparound provider.

Difficulty: ✵ ✵ = Moderate
Topic: Career-long learning
Practice Behavior: Engage in career-long learning

_____

_____

22. You notice that you are very anxious and intimidated when around judges and attorneys and that you lack sufficient knowledge regarding the court system. The best method to lessen your anxiety and increase your knowledge is to:

a. Google the topic that you are interested in.
b. Research information regarding in-service trainings, Continuing Education Units (CEUs), or distance education courses that address your educational needs.

    c. Locate a conference on forensic social work and attend one of their annual meetings.

    d. Ask your supervisor for pamphlets on the court system.

Difficulty: ✦✦ = Moderate

Topic: Advocate for the client

Practice Behavior: Engage in career-long learning

_____

_____

23. Clarks Counseling Agency (CCA), refers JD, a first-time convicted pedophile. Prior to your accepting this client, you have a detailed conversation with the referring attorney, Mr. Smith, who informs you of the challenges that you might face with JD and the shame and denial that you might experience with him. You remember the situation with an earlier client and begin to reflect back on the challenges that you faced and the mistakes that you made. JD comes to your office and complains that he is just depressed and doesn't need treatment. You would first:

    a. Call the attorney and state that he is untreatable.

    b. Tell him what the attorney revealed to you.

    c. Assure JD that everything will be completely confidential.

    d. Refer him to a psychologist.

Difficulty: ✦✦ = Moderate

Topic: Professional communication

Practice Behavior: Demonstrate professional demeanor in behavior, appearance, and communication

_____

_____

24. Kelly, a Child Protective Services (CPS) worker in your county, calls you regarding 10-year-old Chris. Kelly removed Chris from the home of convicted pedophile JD and placed him in foster care. Chris is acting out and hits another child in the foster home. The foster care mother contacts Kelly, and she in turn contacts you at Dell Counseling Agency. You, the social worker, should first:

    a. Talk with Chris about his behavior and then remove him from foster care.

    b. Assess the other children in the home for risk and then advocate for services for Chris.

    c. Have the foster care mother attend parenting classes and then remove Chris from foster care.

    d. Talk with Chris about his behavior.

Difficulty: ✻ = Easy

Topic: Advocate

Practice Behavior: Advocate for client access to the services of social work

---

25. Lamar is involuntarily committed to a psychiatric hospital because of alleged attempts to commit suicide. He refuses to take his medication because he obstinately reports that he never had a plan to hurt himself and that it was just a prank. The social worker should:

    a. Encourage the family to help the patient receive meds.

    b. Discharge the patient.

    c. Remember the client's self-determination.

    d. Check to see if it's state mandated for the patient to receive meds and investigate his allegations.

Difficulty: ✻ ✻ = Moderate

Topic: Advocate for client

Practice Behavior: Advocate for client access to the services of social work

---

26. Maude, an eighty-nine-year-old woman, lives alone. Her neighbor Ruby becomes concerned about a smell coming from Maude's apartment and emails her niece Joan, who works at the County Social Service Agency. Joan makes a home visit to Maude's' apartment and observes that although Maude uses a walker and takes care of herself, and that the apartment is cluttered and dirty but livable. Joan observes that Maude is assertive and welcomes some help. Joan agrees to help Maude. Joan's best approach to ensure the best services for Maude is to:

    a. Ask her aunt Ruby to contact a group of her neighbors to help Maude.

    b. Leave information with Maude about available services.

    c. Make contact with several home management volunteer cleaning services that she has used for other clients.

d. Contact Maude's family.

Difficulty: ✵ = Easy
Topic: Advocate
Practice Behavior: Advocate for client access to the services of social work

---

27. David confers together with his colleagues. He interacts and considers their counsel on certain cases, as well as gives advice that often leads to action. David is essentially providing:

   a. Supervision.
   b. Inspection with authority.
   c. Consultation.
   d. Communication.

Difficulty: ✵ = Easy
Topic: Consultation
Practice Behavior: Use of supervision and consultation

---

28. Mariah has power of attorney for her ninety-two-year-old father Gary, whom she has been taking care of in her home. Gary has had a stroke, and Mariah says she can no longer take care of him. She is unhappy, discontented, miserable, and distressed. Her older brother Milton wants her to continue to care for their father. She is unyielding that she will not continue. As the social worker on the case, you would first:

   a. Discuss this issue with the brother, Milton.
   b. Work with Mariah to reevaluate her decision.
   c. Tour nursing homes with Mariah.
   d. Explore more options for home care.

Difficulty: ✵ ✵ = Moderate
Topic: Advocate for client
Practice Behavior: Advocate for client access to the services of social work

29. You are a new MSW employed at Victory Agency. A couple, Yolanda and Adam, are place on your caseload. Their four-year-old daughter Angel has been kept alive by a respirator for the last six days. They want to terminate this treatment. You have recently lost your four-year-old niece to a lung disease and have not quite recovered from that loss. As their social worker, you would first:

   a. Contact a "right to die" organization on their behalf.
   b. Refer them to someone with experience in this field.
   c. Explore their decision with them.
   d. Explore their feelings.

   Difficulty: ✲ ✲ ✲ = Challenging
   Topic: Boundaries
   Practice Behavior: Attend to professional roles and boundaries

   _____

   _____

30. Florida has been married for a year and a half to George. She has refused to have sex with him ever since their wedding. She has intercourse only when he forces her, and she disassociates during that time. You have personally been in a similar situation with your spouse and have been seeking professional counseling for years. As their social worker, the best approach to this situation is to:

   a. Refer her to a physician for a physical.
   b. Explore her past history of sexual abuse.
   c. Check her into a mental hospital.
   d. Refer her to a professional sex therapist.

   Difficulty: ✲ ✲ ✲ = Challenging
   Topic: Boundaries
   Practice Behavior: Attend to professional roles and boundaries

   _____

   _____

Essay Questions

1. Explain how your professional identity is enhanced by learning the history of social work.

2. Explain what advocating for client access to the services of social work means to you.

3. How do you practice personal reflection and self-correction to ensure continual professional development in social work?

4. What is the importance of attending to professional roles and boundaries in social work? Provide two examples of how this is done.

5. Who were Dorcas Bowles, Florence Hollis, and Leon Chestang, and what is the correlation between their contributions to social work education and your professional identity development?

6. Identify and explain three methods by which social workers can engage in career-long learning beyond their postgraduate level of education.

7. Expound upon your understanding regarding the following statement: "Social workers must demonstrate professional demeanor through appearance."

8. Explain why advocating for clients' rights for service is more than just providing a list of needed services or agency names.

9. Discuss four of the seven areas that speak to the importance of affiliations and orientations as you learn how to advocate for client access to social work services.

10. Explain why your personal reflection and self-correction are rooted in your in understanding of your attributes and increasing your self-awareness.

11. Explain why Jane Addams could have been seen as an initiator, why Bertha Capen Reynolds was a social advocate, and why Whitney M. Young, Jr. played the role of activist, and describe their individual contributions to the profession of social work.

12. How do you see social workers demonstrating professional demeanor in behavior at your current placement?

Role-Play Exercise: Who Am I and What Is It that I Do?

Actions and responses to the role-play "Who Am I and What Is It that I Do?" will vary and depend on your individual characteristics, personal experience, and professional knowledge and are from your own perspective. Learn and enjoy!

You have recently graduated from your MSW program, and some family members, several of your closest friends, and a number of your colleagues from other professional disciplines are questioning your decision to become a social worker. They are unaware of what you do and why you do it, and they devalue your degree. Your decisions are questioned and second-guessed by members of your professional team, and you often times find yourself defending the profession and your actions as a social worker.

This role-play exercise can take place in either a professional formal setting or a relaxed casual setting. The minimum number of participants is four: (1) social worker, (2) social worker colleague, (3) friend, (4) colleague from other discipline. Participants (1) and (2) are pro-social work, while participants (3) and (4) are anti–social work.

Practice with MySocialWorkLab

Visit **MySocialWorkLab** at www.mysocialworklab.com to watch these competency-based videos.

Watch

Professional Identity—**Professional Demeanor**

Professional Identity—**Professional Roles and Boundaries**

Professional Identity—**Advocating for the Client**

References

DuBois, B., & Miley, K. K. (2011). *Social work: An empowering profession* (7th Ed.). Boston: Pearson Education/Allyn & Bacon.

Johnson, L. C., & Yanca, S. J. (2010). *Social work practice: A generalist approach* (10th Ed.). Boston: Allyn & Bacon.

Sabey, M., & Gafner. G. (1996, September). Boundaries in the workplace. *Health Care Supervisor,* 15(1), 36–40. Veterans Affair Medical Center, Tucson, AZ, PMID: 101059638 [PubMed – indexed for Medline].

Smith, M. K. (2005). *The functions of supervision, the encyclopedia of informal education.* Last update: September 3, 2009.

Suppes, M. A., & Wells, C. C. (2009). *The social work experience: An introduction to social work and social welfare* (5th Ed.). Boston: Allyn & Bacon.

2

ETHICAL PRACTICE

CSWE EPAS **2.1.2** *Apply social work ethical principles to guide professional practice*

Ethical practice is the second core competency of the 2008 Educational Policy and Accreditation Standards (EPAS) and presents a firm foundation to build upon as an advanced or second year social work student. This core competency stresses the importance of applying and utilizing social work ethical principles in an effort to guide your professional practice and provide a set core of necessary knowledge, values, and skills by which to obtain it. Understanding the relevance of social work ethical principles and the application of its values during your advanced or second year is not only vitally important to your academic achievement in the classroom, but also crucial for your practicum success in your field placement agencies.

You will also learn that you have an obligation to conduct yourself ethically and responsibly in carrying out the National Association of Social Work (NASW) Code of Ethics and that you must, at all times, engage in ethical decision making. You must not only be aware of the ethical principles, but also secure steps by which to apply them in the field, all of which you will learn and develop some degree of confidence in using them during your advanced or second year. This confidence will ultimately add to your success as professional social workers following graduation from your perspective MSW programs. You will further your understanding and knowledge of the value base of the profession of social work, its ethical standards, and the relevant policies that will help shape your field experiences in your perspective agencies and ultimately direct your professional practice.

As an advanced or second year student, you will become more aware of the importance of the operational practice behaviors of the core competency, ethical practice. You will learn methods that will allow you to recognize and manage your personal values in a way that allows professional values to guide practice.

You will learn how to make better ethical decisions by applying the standards of the NASW Code of Ethics and, when applicable, the International Federation of Social Workers/International Association of Schools of Social Work Ethics in Social Work, Statements of Principles. As an advanced or second year social work student, you will learn how to tolerate some degree of ambiguity in resolving ethical conflicts and how to apply strategies of ethical reasoning to arrive at principled decisions. The techniques you learn will be a continuation of your foundation-year coursework and field experiences and will prove valuable in your pursuit of fair and equitable treatment for your cohorts, colleagues, and clients as an advanced social work student.

RECOGNIZING AND MANAGING PERSONAL AND PROFESSIONAL VALUES

As an advanced or second year social work student, you will recognize that quite often personal morals and professional values overlap causing the management of the two to become overwhelming. You will learn that decisions, in part, are shaped by personal values, which in turn can form your beliefs, emotions, and attitudes. *Values* are those things that are important to or prized by people and that determine which goals and actions they may evaluate as "good." More than just emotional responses to circumstances or merely doing that which feels good, values are central to thought processes that we are not often consciously aware. When values are shared by all members of a profession they are astonishingly important tools for making decisions, evaluating feasible outcomes of anticipated actions, selecting among alternatives, and putting people "on the same page of understanding" regarding what a profession collectively considers important.

You will learn during your advanced or second year that the professional social worker functions within both personal and professional milieus and that personal value can affect your professional styles of intervention and the skills you utilize with your client base. They can also influence the techniques and methods you adopt to accomplish your professional goals, which in turn can affect clients' reactions to your efforts. You will learn your practice in field agencies will be influenced by a system of personal and professional values and by combining your personal values with your professional ethics, you will work toward assisting clients in enhancing their social functioning. By enhancing clients' social functioning, you may possibly prevent the development of social problems such as the disproportionality of children of color in the child welfare system, childhood obesity, and unequal access to healthcare.

Your perspective MSW program will be unable to teach you personal values. They are intricately part of your moral fiber. What you will learn as an advanced or second year MSW student is how to identify the strengths and challenges of some of your personal values. You will learn that personal value systems can be multifaceted composite networks that can develop individually or collectively and are often abstract terms. However, social workers share a common set of values that exist in the form of the NASW Code of Ethics that require adherence to a set of professional values. Social work is a values-based profession with professional shared core values such as: (1) service, (2) social justice, (3) dignity and worth of the person, (4) the importance of human relationships, (5) integrity, and (6) competence, which are inherent in all aspects of social work practice (NASW Code of Ethics, revised by the 2008 NASW Delegate Assembly).

You gained some general understanding of these during your foundation year; and you will further your learning of these six core values during your advanced or second year. However, a brief look at them reveals that *service* (as a value) is the hallmark of the social work profession, is the primary goal of its workers, and is valued over self-interest. *Social justice,* though generally difficult to define as a value in social work is concerned with equal justice in all aspects of society, particularly for marginalized groups such as those who have experienced discrimination, poverty, and prejudice. *Dignity and worth of the person* is a valued ethical principle in which social workers respect and treat each person in a caring way and are mindful of individual differences and promote self-determination. The *importance of human relationships* seeks to express the importance of human relationships to human development and social change in the helping process. *Integrity* is central to the helping relationship as social workers strive to be honest and respectful of clients' rights. Lastly, *competence* is a social worker's commitment to be knowledgeable, well informed, and skilled in their service delivery.

MAKING ETHICAL DECISIONS

Understanding the correlation between values and ethics are central to your ethical decision-making process. You will further understand that your ethical decision making is directly related to your ethical behavior. Ethical behavior can include actions that support moral responsibilities and commitment to the standards for practice as prescribed by the Code of Ethics (DuBois & Miley, 2011). As an operational statement of the central values of the social work profession, the NASW Code of Ethics will guide you at your practicums and later direct practice after graduating from your perspective MSW programs. You will continue to learn how ethics relate to that which is identified or considered "right" and generate standards that direct your decision-making process and represent "values in action" (Levy, 1979, p. 233).

Ethics represent values in action as well as behavioral expectations associated with social work responsibility (Levy, 1979). Conrad and Glenn (1976) identified two types of ethics that are central to the ethical decision-making process: microethics and macroethics. *Microethics* relates to those ideals and values that direct practice, whereas *macroethics* are concerned with organizational arrangements, values, and ethical principles that bring about and guide social policies. Morales, Sheafor, and Scott (2012) identify two central functions that values play in making ethical decisions: instrumental values and terminal values. *Instrumental values* are instrumental in the development of the moral or ethical guidelines that assist in defining conduct both personally and professionally, while *terminal values* refer to the final analysis of what you want to accomplish. Examples of instrumental values that direct ethical decision making could be how we should or should not behave; while terminal values could be ensuring that all pregnant mothers receive good prenatal care regardless of the ability to pay or ensuring secure housing for all people regardless of socioeconomic status. Values and ethics are central to the profession of social work and are imperative for the profession's mission.

TOLERATING AMBIGUITY IN RESOLVING ETHICAL CONFLICTS

When working with clients, you will learn that you may never be sure of what has gone on in their pasts or will happen in their futures, as there are many unknowns and some degree of ambiguity is inevitable. In your advanced or second year at your perspective MSW programs, you will further your understanding of your capacity to deal with ambiguity and learn methods for tolerating some degree of doubt in resolving ethical conflicts both personally and professionally. Ambiguity is uncomfortable, and uncertainty creates tension. The NASW Code of Ethics outlines the ethical standards that you will rely on. These national standards will aid you in your understanding of ethical issues and will be instrumental in the process of resolving them. They are the most tangible expressions of the profession's guidelines. There are many techniques for how to tolerate ambiguity, however, when working with ambiguity in resolving ethical conflict, it is helpful to have (1) the capability to ask for help; and (2) belief in the ability to change.

To increase your effectiveness while struggling with ambiguity, your *capability to ask for help* and a positive attitude will increase your tolerance in resolving ethical conflicts. In your practicum experience, you will learn that many of your clients might be resistant to change and fearful of the unknown regardless of their current situations. A powerful *belief in the ability to grow and change* is another strategy for tolerating ambiguity in resolving ethical conflicts. You will learn that when a client's right to control his or her own behavior clashes with another set of rights, conflict is inevitable. When tolerating ambiguity in resolving ethical conflicts, it is important to consider self-determination. Self-determination is the client's right to determine his or her own life plan without interference.

Eventually, you will experience ethical conflict in your professional journey. Some forms of ethical conflict might arise from differences between you and your cohorts, your clients, and your college regarding attitudes toward politics, religion, sexuality, culture, social class, time orientation, or the environment, or concerning beliefs about human nature. You will learn that ambiguity which results in ethical conflicts can cause value conflicts and dilemmas. While all social workers share common beliefs that are fundamental values of the profession, they also hold differing beliefs that sometimes stem from conflicting personal values. A large part of resolving ethical conflicts is simply to know that they exist. *Value conflicts* are disagreements brought about by differences in people's values; *value dilemmas* are situations in which competing values make it difficult, if not impossible, to determine the correct choice (Morales, Sheafor & Scott, 2012).

APPLYING ETHICAL REASONING STRATEGIES TO ARRIVE AT PRINCIPLED DECISIONS

There are many ways to apply ethical reasoning strategies in an effort to arrive at principled decisions in the ethical practice of social work. The following three methods, if adopted, can assist you in that process: (1) understanding the professional principles of social work; (2) securing a model for ethical decision making; and (3) subscribing to the six core values that drive the profession. As advanced social work student practitioners, you will continue to learn that ethics conceptually form your way of thinking as well as tangibly directing your actions through principles of social work practice (DuBois & Miley, 2011). The acronym KNOW represents a four-step plan which serves as a solid foundational understanding for applying ethical reasoning strategies: (1) knowledge of access to resources; (2) nonjudgmental attitudes; (3) objectivity; and (4) willing acceptance (DuBois & Miley, 2011).

Knowledge of access to resources is a precondition to the emergence of principled decisions, however, inadequate resources limit solutions. *Nonjudgmental attitudes* are fundamental to successful working relationships and form the basis of clients' dignity and self-worth. *Objectivity* is holding an exploratory or investigative attitude toward circumstances and conditions without bias; you will learn that objectivity can be affected by many factors not limited to your academic knowledge and/or your belief systems. Lastly, *willing acceptance* of the client suggests an authentic concern allowing you to listen receptively and show mutual respect (DuBois & Miley, 2011).

You will arrive at a principled decisions by studying and reviewing various models of ethical decision making that exist for this helping profession. Ethical decision making involves both the social worker and the client and is not done in isolation. The first step of many models is to identify the problems or potential issues which created the need to adopt an ethical decision process. Acknowledgment of the problem and identification of the parties involved will aid in the decision-making process and resolution of the problem allowing relevant values to the problem be identified. Identifying and selecting alternate intervention strategies and possible courses of action are the steps to take before implementing the strategy (Corey, Corey & Callanan, 2011). This can be accomplished by reviewing the NASW Code of Ethics.

PRACTICE ETHICAL BEHAVIORS AND ASSESS OUTCOMES

This section will help further your understanding of the behaviors to the 2008 CSWE EPAS 2.1.2 *Apply social work ethical principles to guide professional practice*: (1) recognize and manage personal values in a way that allows professional values to guide practice; (2) make ethical decisions by applying standards of the National Association of Social Workers Code of Ethics and, as applicable, of the International Federations of Social Workers/International Association of Schools of Social Work, Statement of Principles; (3) tolerate ambiguity in resolving ethical conflicts; and (4) apply strategies of ethical reasoning to arrive at principled decisions. Each question that follows will test your application of the practice behaviors and your ability to think critically regarding their function. The questions are deliberately varied and randomly placed regarding the four ethical practice practice behaviors.

Multiple Choice

(Note: On the lines below each multiple-choice question, explain why you chose that particular answer.)

Difficulty Scale: ✲ = Easy   ✲ ✲ = Moderate   ✲ ✲ ✲ = Challenging

1. Phillip is a second year social work student interning at Pilgrims' Rest, an agency that provides services to men who are victims of spousal abuse. Over the last couple of weeks, the agency has experienced an influx of clients. Phillip has noticed that his personal belief that men are stronger than and superior to women has conflicted with his professional values and the mission of Pilgrims' Rest, particularly with the new client Dennis. Dennis is 6' 7" tall and weighs approximately 370 pounds. Phillip has had a problem with Dennis and has come to the conclusion that he just doesn't like him and finds internal conflict impeding delivery of services to him. The best thing Philip could do regarding Dennis is to:

    a. seek therapy to find out why he dislikes Dennis.
    b. tell Dennis of his dislike and his internal struggles to deliver services to him.
    c. speak to his supervisor and/or university field liaison so he can better understand his internal conflicts toward Dennis.
    d. refer Dennis to another social work intern.

    Difficulty: ✲ ✲ = Moderate
    Topic: Managing personal values
    Practice Behavior: Recognizing and managing personal and professional values to guide practice

    _____

    _____

2. Elizabeth, a recent graduate of an MSW program, works at Morton's Care, a local hospice agency in your county. She is loved by many of the residents at Morton's Care, particularly those who have few or no relatives. Charitie, a dying patient, wants to include Elizabeth in her will, because she feels that Elizabeth has been very nice to her and takes care of her better than her relatives, who seldom visit because they live out of state. The initial thing Elizabeth should do in response to this situation is:

    a. Plan to accept the money and donate it to charity.
    b. Tell the family of Charitie's plan.
    c. Explore with the patient how else the money could be spent.

d. Explore Charitie's reasons for wanting to include her in her will.

Difficulty: ✵ ✵ = Moderate
Topic: Making ethical decisions
Practice Behavior: Make ethical decisions by applying standards of NASW

_____

_____

3. Florence is in her first semester of her second year of a MSW program, interning at a state-agency policy department. She has gone to her supervisor for help. She is questioning her choice of social work as a career and doesn't feel that she can follow all of the policy and standards of the NASW Code of Ethics because she has experienced so many violations of them as an intern. She also feels that she is not dependable enough to be a social worker. The least appropriate response by her supervisor would be to:

   a. Help her identify her specific concerns.
   b. Problem-solve for her.
   c. Refer her to a peer support group.
   d. Refer her to the director of her MSW program.

Difficulty: ✵ = Easy
Topic: Ambiguity
Practice Behavior: Tolerate ambiguity in resolving ethical conflicts

_____

_____

4. Patrice has given her three-year-old daughter, Aretha, and seven-year-old son, Franklin, to her neighbor Stephanie to take care of while she is in an inpatient mental-health treatment program for depression due to a recent divorce. Stephanie is your identical twin's best friend and has been to your home for holiday parties and your children's birthday parties. You work for the Child Protective Services (CPS) in your county and are aware of past allegations of Stephanie abusing her own children. An anonymous report has been received that Patrice's children are being neglected and abused by Stephanie. You, the Child Protective Services worker, should first:

   a. Inform Patrice about the situation.
   b. Remove the children from Stephanie's home.

   c. Speak with Stephanie who is taking care of Patrice's children.

   d. Investigate the allegation.

Difficulty: ✿ ✿ ✿ = Challenging

Topic: Ethical reasoning

Practice Behavior: Applying strategies of ethical reasoning to arrive at principled decisions

_____

_____

5. Jamie is a second year intern at For Blessings Counseling Center. His six-year-old client Farrist wants you to agree not to tell her mother, Martha, if she tells you an important secret. You assure him that you:

   a. will keep what is discussed confidential.

   b. would only tell his mother, Martha, things in his presence.

   c. will not tell his mother anything he tells you without discussing it with him first.

   d. will tell his mother everything he reports.

Difficulty: ✿ ✿ ✿ = Challenging

Topic: Managing personal values

Practice Behavior: Recognize and manage personal values in a way that allows professional values to guide practice

_____

_____

6. You are two weeks from graduating with your MSW, and Laura, a twenty-three-year-old woman who has just been accepted in your MSW program for the upcoming semester, is having a sexual relationship with your four-teen-year-old cousin Allison. According to Allison, she initiated the sexual contact with Laura, and Laura agreed. You should file a suspected child abuse report for which of the following reasons:

   a. Laura is enrolled in a professional program and is in violation of its ethical codes.

   b. Your cousin Allison is under age eighteen and Laura is an adult.

   c. Your cousin initiated the sexual act, but due to it being her first sexual experience, she was not sure the act qualified as sex; however, the twenty-three-year-old knew it was sex.

d. Same-sex relationships are a violation of the NASW Code of Ethics.

Difficulty: ✧✧ = Moderate
Topic: Managing personal values
Practice Behavior: Recognize and manage personal values

_____

_____

7. Genevieve is an LMSW working with you at Better Homes for Boys, a foster home for male juvenile second-time offenders that is owned by your great aunt Bessie. She admits to you that she has caught a sexually transmitted disease from one of the twelve-year-old residents and has narrowed down the transmitter of the disease to Buddy or JoJo. You have been friends with Genevieve since you both graduated from your MSW program five years ago. In this case you should:

   a. Ask Genevieve for the names of every boy that she has had sex with at Better Homes and then report her to the state regulatory board and provide the names to the board so they can investigate the matter.
   b. Report Genevieve to the state regulatory board without giving the client's name to the board.
   c. Immediately educate Genevieve regarding the ethical ramifications for having sex with minors and demand that she resign from Better Homes and never practice social work again, because you have an ethical duty to protect your profession.
   d. Consult with Buddy and JoJo before taking further action, in order to determine if the sex was consensual.

Difficulty: ✧✧ = Moderate
Topic: Ethical decisions
Practice Behavior: Making ethical decisions by applying standards of the NASW Code of Ethics

_____

_____

8. You have been treating Abigail, a young woman who was charged with the abuse of her nine-year-old son, Ryan. She has now met all the goals of her treatment plan, has been very cooperative, and attended all of her treatment sessions. Her son is about to be returned to her from foster care when she tells you that she is three months pregnant by her brother-in-law. As her caseworker, you should:

   a. Ask your client to return after the child is born and consider allowing her sister to adopt the baby, since she is unable to have her own children.

b. Return her to conditional custody of her son and monitor carefully.

c. Arrange for continuing foster care for her nine-year-old because of her immoral sexual behavior with a married man.

d. Return full custody of her son to her, since he has met all her treatment goals, and close the case.

Difficulty: ⁂ ⁂ = Moderate

Topic: Managing personal values

Practice Behavior: Recognizing and managing personal and professional values to guide practice.

_____

_____

9. Jill, a past client of yours, reports you to the Board of Social Work Examiners. In terms of the ethics of the situation, you should first:

a. Have some of your peers who find your work to be professional speak on your behalf before the board.

b. Turn over your treatment plan and diagnosis of the client to the board.

c. Turn over your process notes and impressions of the client to the board.

d. Due to confidentiality issues, decline to give the board any information.

Difficulty: ⁂ = Easy

Topic: Ambiguity

Practice Behavior: Tolerate ambiguity in resolving ethical conflicts

_____

_____

10. You are an intern at Fair Family Counseling Center and have been shadowing your agency supervisor, Fonzie, an LMSW who is also the agency director. You observed him on more than one occasion creating notes that did not accurately reflect his actions with certain clients on his caseload who lived in potentially dangerous areas of the city. He recorded in his notes that he had face-to-face meetings with several of his clients at their homes, when he actually had only phone contacts with several and Skyped with those who had the technology to do so. The most appropriate action for you to take is to:

a. Follow up with a face-to-face meeting with the clients in an effort to protect the future of your intern opportunity with Fair Family Counseling Center.

b. Discuss your concerns about moral considerations with Fonzie.

c. Discuss your concerns about potential ethical-legal considerations with your school mentor/field advisor and/or university field director.

d. Nothing, because the agency director has not really violated any ethical principles, as he did make contact with the clients.

Difficulty: ✵ ✵ ✵ = Challenging

Topic: Ethical reasoning

Practice Behavior: Applying strategies of ethical reasoning to arrive at principled decisions

_____

_____

11. Logan is a LMSW who works as a child welfare advocate with a private agency that provides social services to clients not served well by your local state agency. Thomas, a lawyer for one of your clients, calls you for information about a mutual client hours before the court date. You are on a vacation in London but answer Thomas's call because you are good friends. You state to him that you are not sure if he has ever submitted any requests for release of written information, let alone for the particular client he is inquiring about. Thomas says the client has signed a release. You should:

a. Cooperate and give the information over the phone, because personally you are good friends, and professionally, he is a lawyer sworn to abide by his ethical code.

b. Wait for Thomas to subpoena you.

c. Give the information only after you received a written release from Thomas or are confident that you have one on file.

d. Call the client and check with him.

Difficulty: ✵ ✵ = Moderate

Topic: Ethical reasoning

Practice Behavior: Applying strategies of ethical reasoning to arrive at principled decisions

_____

_____

12. Jennifer is the mother of your twenty-one-year-old client Bryan. You and she use the same hair salon, and while you are both there for your appointments, Jennifer engages you in conversation and asks to be included in the ongoing treatment of her son. You should:

a. Include her in the ongoing treatment with her son Bryan.

b. Tell Jennifer that you will ask her son Bryan to speak with her.

c. Tell Jennifer to discuss the possibility with her son.
d. Refuse to see her.

Difficulty: ✸✸ = Moderate

Topic: Ethical decisions

Practice Behavior: Making ethical decisions by applying standards of the NASW Code of Ethics

_____

_____

13. The nursing staff at a local hospital where you are interning as a medical social worker complains about the behavior of Martin, a thirty-three-year-old recent veteran amputee. He is egotistical and intolerable, and he is not complying with the department program. It is very easy to dislike him and provide him with substandard service because of his attitude. The nursing staff asks for your help with Martin. You should:

a. Ask the doctor about Martin's psychological condition.
b. Speak with Martin.
c. Ask the nursing staff about their concerns.
d. Confront Martin about this behavior.

Difficulty: ✸✸ = Moderate

Topic: Ethical decisions

Practice Behavior: Making ethical decisions by applying standards of the NASW Code of Ethics

_____

_____

14. Jimmy, a social worker, accepts the referral of a competent patient in the hospital who wants to establish a living will. The social worker should:

a. Speak with the family first.
b. Assist the patient with his wishes for his own medical treatment.
c. Call an attorney.
d. Check with the nursing staff to see whether they would honor the will or not.

Difficulty: ✸✸ = Moderate

Topic: Ethical decisions

Practice Behavior: Making ethical decisions by applying standards of the NASW Code of Ethics

_____

_____

15. Your son is playing basketball with a group of eight-year-old boys while you observe a weekly supervised visit at a local church approved by the Department of Family and Children Services. Your son gets into a fight with another boy, and two of the other boys take sides. What should you do first?

    a. Report the incident to the other parents.
    b. Put them in an activity where they can do something together.
    c. Set up weekly group therapy sessions.
    d. Decide who was right and encourage others to go along.

    Difficulty: ✳ ✳ = Moderate
    Topic: Managing personal values
    Practice Behavior: Recognizing and managing personal and professional values to guide practice

    _____

    _____

16. You are a director of field education for a MSW program. Ava, a student, has come to you stating that she is having relationship difficulties with her male agency supervisor, Michael. Michael also contacts you. He reports that he is having problems with Ava. The best approach for you to take is to:

    a. Call Ava back and tell her that Michael, the agency supervisor, has some questions about her effectiveness.
    b. Ask both parties to meet with you in an attempt to discuss their concerns.
    c. Refer them to the director of the MSW program.
    d. Let them resolve their issues on their own.

    Difficulty: ✳ = Easy
    Topic: Ambiguity
    Practice Behavior: Tolerate ambiguity in resolving ethical conflicts

    _____

    _____

17. Parker is a social work intern in an adolescent shelter and is assigned to Adam, a fourteen-year-old male who has run away from his family. He does not wish for his family to know his where he is. When asked about his reasons for leaving home, Adam says that he has problems with his father, but does not volunteer any additional information. Parker would first:

    a. Notify the parents that Adam is at the shelter and request that they come in for a family interview.
    b. Share with Adam that no subject is off limits and encourage him to discuss any offensive or unpleasant subjects.

c. Interview the parents.

d. Tell Adam that when he is ready to talk, a social worker is available.

Difficulty: ✦✦ = Moderate

Topic: Ethical reasoning

Practice Behavior: Applying strategies of ethical reasoning to arrive at principled decisions

_____

_____

18. Vincent, a social worker, starts a home-based business selling discounted phone and wireless internet services. He is passionate about helping people save money on these services. His supervisor, Mitchell, soon learns that Vincent is sending email correspondence to clients and co-workers whom he knows struggle financially because of their expensive home utilities and is personally soliciting orders from staff and clients. The supervisor should:

a. Do nothing.

b. Suggest that Vincent ask the agency director for permission to market his products.

c. Inform Vincent that there are ethical prohibitions against using his professional position to advance his private business interests.

d. Require that Vincent relinquish his business interests if he wishes to continue working at the agency.

Difficulty: ✦✦ = Moderate

Topic: Managing personal values

Practice Behavior: Recognizing and managing personal and professional values to guide practice

_____

_____

19. Mason, a social worker employed in a residential group home for boys, learns that Jeremy, a fellow employee, has multiple convictions for sexual molestation of young male children. The agency is unaware of his history, even though he was asked pre-employment questions about previous convictions. Sexual offenses automatically disqualify applicants for employment at the group home. Mason's professional and ethical obligations are best met by:

a. Immediately notify the responsible agency manager of the situation.

b. Saying and doing nothing, because he is good friends with Jeremy.

c. Urging Jeremy to reveal his history to management.

d. Notify Jeremy's the man's probation officer.

Difficulty: ✿✿ = Moderate

Topic: Ethical decisions

Practice Behavior: Making ethical decisions by applying standards of the NASW Code of Ethics

_____

_____

20. Anthony, an agency board member for ABC International Social Services, calls Pierre, a senior clinical supervisor, and asks him to visit him at his office to discuss a confidential question concerning the executive director's competence, behavior, and performance. Pierre's best professional response is:

a. "I don't think I should meet with you, Anthony Pierre."

b. "If you have a question, shouldn't it be raised with the board, who can then authorize an official evaluation?"

c. "I'd rather discuss it over the phone than at your office."

d. "Why don't you speak with the assistant director about this matter as he could possibly give you inside information that I cannot provide?"

Difficulty: ✿✿ = Moderate

Topic: Ethical reasoning

Practice Behavior: Applying strategies of ethical reasoning to arrive at principled decisions

_____

_____

Essay Questions

1. Discuss the importance of applying and utilizing social work ethical principles as a student in your classroom setting, and provide an example of when you experienced and/or witnessed both a poor use and a good use of ethics.

2. Define values, and explain what part they play, if any, in our belief systems and how they affect our personal and professional selves. In your answer, identify the strengths and challenges of some of your personal values and professional values.

3. Identify two examples of when your personal morals and professional values overlapped, and discuss the impact on you and your family personally as well as on your cohorts, clients, and colleagues professionally.

4. Discuss how the NASW Code of Ethics addresses the core values of the profession, and identify and discuss three of the six core values with which you struggle.

5. Discuss the correlation between values and ethics in your ethical decision-making and the way in which they affect your ethical behavior both personally and professionally.

6. Discuss why the application and utilization of social work ethical principles are relevant and important as a student within your interaction in your field placement agency settings. Provide two examples each of how you experienced and/or witnessed both a poor and a good use of ethics in an effort to guide your professional judgment.

7. Identify and discuss the two types of ethics that are central to the ethical decision-making process and provide an example of each that you either experienced or witnessed.

8. Discuss how the acronym KNOW relates to the application of ethical reasoning in an attempt to arrive at principled decisions in the ethical practice of social work.

Role-Play Exercise: Ethical Practice in the Classroom

Actions within and responses to the role-play will vary and depend on your individual characteristics, personal experience, and professional knowledge and rely on your own perspective. Learn and enjoy!

There is only one week of class work before the final exam week of the first semester of your advanced/second year in your MSW program. You see your professor in the hall and remind her to post the study guide for the upcoming final exam. She thanks you and tells you that she will go directly to her office and post it on the class-dedicated website. In her haste, the professor accidentally posts the final exam instead of the study guide. You know that you are the first to get the post because the post time shows in two minutes after the professor posted it. What do you do?

Consider the following scenarios in your role-play.

> Scenario #1—You are struggling in the class and must get a passing grade in order to stay in the program.
> Scenario #2—You are the leader of a study group and many of your cohorts depend on your notes.
> Scenario #3—You call one of your cohorts whom you trust and share with him about the accidental posting of the final because you are not sure what to do.

All participants must role-play what they would do in this situation to demonstrate a decision based on their personal and professional values.

Practice with MySocialWorkLab

Visit **MySocialWorkLab** at www.mysocialworklab.com to watch these competency-based videos.

Watch

Ethical Practice—**Recognizing Personal Values**

Ethical Practice—**Managing Personal Values: The Code of Ethics**

Ethical Practice—**Tolerating Ambiguity in Resolving Conflicts**

References

Conrad, W., & Glenn, W. (1976). *The effective voluntary board of directors: What it is and how it works.* Chicago: Swallow Press.

Corey, G., Corey, M., & Callanan, P. (2011). *Issues and ethics in the helping profession* (8th ed.). Belmont, CA: Brooks/Cole, Cengage Learning.

DuBois, B., and Miley, K. K. (2011). *Social work: An empowering profession* (7th ed.). Boston: Pearson Education/Allyn & Bacon.

Levy, C. S. (1979). *Social work ethics.* New York: Human Sciences Press.

Morales, A. T., Sheafor, B. W., & Scott, M. E. (2012). *Social work: A Profession of many faces* (Updated 12th ed.). Boston: Pearson Education/Allyn & Bacon.

National Association of Social Workers (NASW). Approved 1996, revised 2008. *Code of ethics for social workers.* Washington, D.C.: NASW.

3

CRITICAL
THINKING

CSWE EPAS **2.1.3** *Apply critical thinking to inform and communicate professional judgments*

Critical thinking is the third core competency of the 2008 EPAS and provides a solid foundation to build upon as an advanced or second year social work student. Critical thinking techniques learned from this competency are outstanding tools for decision making and are particularly important for social workers because they will teach you to question theories and challenge assumptions about people's behaviors and actions. As a core competency, critical thinking seeks to improve the quality of the social worker's professional opinions, ethical decisions, and reasoned discernment. As an advanced or second year student, you will begin to understand the science behind critical thinking that facilitates social workers in becoming more knowledgeable about the principles of logic as they seek to inform and communicate professional judgment in practice. You will recognize the art of scientific inquiry as you augment critical thinking techniques with your creativity and curiosity in your classes, with your cohorts, and in your field agencies.

In your foundation year, you learned and practiced the art of critical thinking and adopted related knowledge and skill sets in everyday life, in the classroom, and practicum settings. However, as advanced or second year students, you will begin to distinguish, appraise, and integrate multiple sources of knowledge, research, and practice wisdom because of your ability to apply critical thinking to inform professional judgment. You will learn that critical thinking also requires the synthesis and communication of relevant information as you refine your capacity to analyze models of assessment, prevention, intervention, and evaluation. Lastly, you will demonstrate effective oral and written communication in working with individuals, families, groups, organizations, communities, and colleagues as you apply critical thinking to inform and communicate professional judgment. You will enjoy this process as you learn that critical thinking also requires the synthesis and communication of relevant information.

DISTINGUISHING, APPRAISING, AND INTEGRATING MULTIPLE SOURCES OF KNOWLEDGE, RESEARCH, AND PRACTICE WISDOM

Though the most basic knowledge of a social worker is analogous, as advanced or second year MSW students, you will further learn that social workers possess knowledgeable backgrounds and that these diverse levels of understanding among social workers vary significantly. These differences depend on the viewing platforms and the level of the program or person categorizing the areas of practice proficiencies. You will further learn as advanced student practitioners that the knowledge that fortifies the techniques and skills that a social worker must possess is broad and depends on your perspective MSW program and its specialization. You will learn that given the opportunity to deliver special services and provide certain programs, it is the responsibility of the social work profession to monitor its members and protect the public against abuses or unethical behavior.

There are four components of *appraising and integrating multiple sources of knowledge* as an advanced or second year social work student. First, you must understand the individuals, families, and organizations within the community in which you work relative to their interactions within the systems that provide social programs and deliver social services. Second, you must recognize the mutual relationship of your client-base regarding the shared degree of difficulties and problematic agency issues and their intersection within the context of their lives. Third, you must have some degree of knowledge regarding issues that largely affect your clients' self-worth, self-esteem, and quality of life, such as (1) adequate supply of safe housing; (2) the quality of education in their communities; and (3) the political and economic climate not only locally, regionally, or nationally, but globally. Lastly, as advanced or second year students, you must recognize the central purposes and roles that social workers carry out from a societal perspective and the benefits and responsibilities thereof. Practice connects clients with the services, while social workers provide the knowledge of various regulations, policies, and procedures that affect the delivery of those services (Groundwater-Smith & Sachs, 2002; Sheafor & Horejsi, 2011).

You will also learn that there are various approaches to appraising and integrating the multiple sources of knowledge and research. This knowledge can be assessed and integrated based on the levels of professional social work practice. You will learn that knowledge appraisal and integration can be done at the four different levels of social work professional practice: (1) basic—BSW, (2) specialized—new MSW, (3) independent—MSW with at least two years of experience, and (4) advanced (NASW, 1981).

You will discover that the *basic level* of professional practice requires skills, theoretical knowledge, and values that you learned during your foundation year if you are a second year student or during your final semesters in your undergraduate liberal arts program. The *specialized level* of professional practice requires a broad conceptual knowledge of research, administration, or planning methods and social problems. At this level, you will demonstrate a mastery of therapeutic techniques of knowledge and skill methods, all of which you will learn as an advanced or second year MSW student. At this level of professional practice, you will possess advanced knowledge and skills specific to your area of specialization (NASW, 1981; Morales, Sheafor & Scott, 2012).

Practice at the *independent level* is training beyond the MSW and focuses more upon your areas of specification. A minimum of two years of postgraduate experience in direct practice, administration, or training competence is required, as is the integration of knowledge, values, and skills of the profession in a specialization. A number of indicators can measure social work practice at this level, such as the Academy of Certified Social Workers (ACSW) or the Qualified Clinical Social Worker (QCSW) credentialing (NASW, 1981; Morales, Sheafor & Scott, 2012). The *advanced level* carries major social and organizational responsibility for professional development, analysis, research, and policy implementation. This level requires proficiency in specific areas, such as administration or policy, or the ability to conduct advanced research studies. This is usually demonstrated through a doctoral degree in social work in addition to the MSW degree. You will learn that NASW has codified these four levels into a classification system with expectations for the practitioner at each level defined and education and experience qualifications specified (Morales, Sheafor & Scott, 2012).

Distinguishing multiple sources of practice wisdom in professional social work practice requires sound judgment in the use of personal/professional, theoretical, and practical knowledge. It is a form of knowledge drawn from personal observations and collective experiences. You will further your understanding of practice wisdom during your advanced or second year as you see its reflective, affective, and experiential qualities and moral/ethical dimensions (Sheafor & Horejsi, 2012; Sternberg, 1990).

Practice wisdom is not necessarily content-based, but is associated with the manner in which knowledge is held and how that knowledge is put to use in exercising judgment. You will learn that practice wisdom combines practical knowledge with sound judgment and thoughtful action—action in which you, the skilled social worker, are exact in utilizing your unique style of drawing from your experiences to enhance the current situations and challenges with your clients, cohorts, and colleagues.

In appraising the multiple sources of practice wisdom, you will begin to understand the invisible elements of practice. Knowledgeable social work professionals who are responsive and attuned to clients convey their professionalism and the hidden dimensions of their practice through the environments they create and the interactions in which they engage. However, many factors contribute to the professional/practical knowledge that is reflected in practice wisdom. As an advanced student practitioner, you will learn that the characteristics of practice wisdom also include an ability to learn from ideas and from the environment, as well as from intuition—that is, being able to see beyond what is spoken, reading between the lines, and interpreting messages gleaned through interactions with social and physical environments (Gambrill & Gibbs, 2009).

While some aspects of who we are may be evident in our actions, we are also involved in very complex decision making as we go about those actions in our efforts to integrate the multiple sources of practice wisdom. You will learn that personal qualities and experiences lie below the surface of our doing. Professional practice draws on these dimensions, as well as on our theoretical/ professional knowledge, as we engage in decision making within our everyday practices. Professional practice and practice wisdom draw on knowledge and experience. Such practice also reflects understandings that have developed not only through experience and through the acquisition of theoretical knowledge, but through reflection and the capacity to appreciate the personal attributes, feelings, attitudes, beliefs, and values that influence actions.

ANALYZING MODELS OF ASSESSMENT, PREVENTION, INTERVENTION, AND EVALUATION

As advanced student practitioners, you will understand the importance of assessment, prevention, intervention, and evaluation and their correlation to the critical thinking process. In your foundation year, you learned the significance of critical thinking for social work; during your advanced or second year, you will learn that social work distinguishes itself from the other helping professions in many ways, one of which concerns dealing with people with problems. You will begin to learn that social workers seek not to problem-solve but to examine the person-in-environment with a concentration on assisting clients in both solving and preventing problem. This is where critical thinking and its relationship to analyzing becomes evident.

Critical thinking means that you learn better ways to think and utilize related knowledge and skills in everyday life that require flexibility of thought and keen, deliberate interest in discovering past and current mistakes in your thinking. As an advanced or second year student, you will learn that critical thinking plays an important role in your professional development as a social worker and impacts on your relationships within the classroom, agency settings, and your environment. The relationship between critical thinking and evidence-based informed practice are two correlations that you see as being practical parts of your everyday lives as well as your professional journeys.

Consider the following scenarios. During a lecture on human behavior, your HBSE professor tells the class that people who are accepting of others will accept them unconditionally, including their differences. Will you believe him because he has a doctoral degree and has taught the class for over twenty years, or simply because he said so? If you do not take his words at face value, what further information will you seek, and why? How will you *evaluate* that data collected? If you analyze it, what impact does it have on you?

Suppose your policy professor tells you that Osama bin Laden and his regime are no longer a threat to U.S. national security because he has been assassinated. Do you agree with him because you see him as the authority on international affairs? Do you accept this idea as truth because it was validated by CNN?

Finally, imagine that the agency supervisor at your practicum site tells you that the wraparound services you recommended for your client were inappropriate for his diagnosis and recommends another wraparound provider. She further tells you that she has worked with clients who have similar diagnoses for years and that the client would not benefit from the services you recommended. Would you follow her recommendation or would you question her decision?

When you consider the aforementioned scenarios or similar ones, you engage in critical thinking. Critical thinking is a developmentally stimulating, focused act that is self-assessing and self-evaluative and oftentimes yields well-reasoned results. You possibly underwent a series of steps in the critical thinking process in making your decision to pursue your MSW, intern at your current agency, or decide on your next course elective. These all are examples and products of critical thinking.

You will learn that a multiplicity of assessment models exist that help identify the strengths and weaknesses or problems of a client or within a client system. An assessment is informed by current human behavior research that emphasizes multidimensional and functional analysis enhanced by qualitative and quantitative tools (O'Hare, 2009). The traditional assessment model attempts to develop rapport and a working relationship that emphasizes integrity, dignity, respect, and trust. This model identifies problems and issues that create difficulties and is usually written in terms of what needs to be resolved. Components of the model include psychosocial history, mental status, level of functioning, clinical assessment, and recommendations and goals for treatment. The strengths-based model assesses the inherent strengths within a client or client system and seeks to build upon those strengths. This model is empowerment that underscores the process of assessment and treatment that removes stigmatizing terms and identifies and reviews the client's positive attributes.

You will learn that there are various levels of intervention and prevention approaches and no one approach fits all practice situations. You will learn that the approach you adopt can depend on your perspective or the manner in which you approach understanding and assessing a client's issue. Morales, Sheafor, and Scott (2012) identified three models of prevention: primary, secondary, and tertiary. *Primary prevention* is when a social worker attempts to modify an environment in an effort to reduce or eliminate social, economic, mental health, and other conditions that may cause or contribute to a client's problems. *Secondary* and *tertiary prevention* are issues that social workers identify can be treated in manners that keep clients' situations from getting worse and situations that help clients cope with conditions that cannot be changed, respectively (Morales, Sheafor & Scott, 2012). Interventions are combinations of skills applied by practitioners, their clients, and collateral participants—such as family members, friends, and teachers—that are implemented for the purpose of reducing symptoms, resolving problems, enhancing adaptive capabilities, and improving the overall psychosocial well-being of the client (O'Hare, 2009).

You will learn that there are many models of intervention in social work; however, in your advanced year, you will further your study and analyze the dynamics of intervention such as family and group therapy. *Family therapy* refers to interventions conducted with some or all members of a family, whereas *group therapy* refers to working with the members of a group of persons who are generally not related in a familial way to one another. You will learn that the key characteristics of social work interventions are (1) the focus on the whole of the person's life, social context, and environment; (2) the capacity to engage quickly with people to establish trust; (3) to consciously move into situations that would be avoided by most people because they are complex and high-risk; and (4) the capacity to manage situations where risks are very finely balanced. An evaluation can be the use of qualitative or quantitative methods to incrementally update the assessment, adjust the intervention, and measure client progress (O'Hare, 2009). In your advanced or second year MSW programs, you will learn that there are many models of evaluation, two of which are direct practice evaluation and process evaluation. *Direct practice evaluation* is the appraisal of interventions and their impact on certain clients, whereas *process evaluation* is geared toward fully understanding how a program works and how it produces its results.

DEMONSTRATING EFFECTIVE INTERPERSONAL COMMUNICATION SKILLS

Communication essentially is the exchange of information between people that defines relationships and occurs across distance in time and space empowering ways of thinking between you, your clients, and those with whom you interact. You will learn that demonstrating effective interpersonal communication skills is essential in the helping professions in general and vitally important to the profession of social work, and it is inescapable for good relationships with clients.

Interpersonal communication is contextual, in that it does not happen in isola-tion, and has three pathways: (1) mental, (2) relational, and (3) social. It is a *men-tal* context, in that it includes who you are and what you bring to the interaction; *relational*, as it concerns your relationships to your clients, cohorts, colleagues, and others; and *social*, because it deals with where you are communicating. Interpersonal skills have a lot to do with communication skills, in that when you interact with others, you always use some form of communication. Some basic components of demonstrating effective interpersonal communication skills are to (1) analyze personal communication style; (2) recognize barriers to commu-nication and select effective techniques to overcome them; and (3) understand active listening behaviors as it relates to effective interpersonal communication.

As an advanced student practitioner, you will begin to understand that to create an effective helping relationship and demonstrate effective interpersonal communication, you must have assertive skills and nonverbal communication skills. *Assertive skills* can be composed of competence and genuineness and can be used to clarify, to express feelings, or to obtain information. *Competence* is having some degree of proficiency in carrying out your professional tasks and activities, while *genuineness* refers to a professional who is real and speaks from the heart. You will learn that human caring is at the very heart of the relation-ship with your clients and should be shown to them at all times. According to Sheafor and Horejsi (2012), you must genuinely care about your clients and they must know that you "really care"; when your clients trust you, they have faith and confidence in your integrity, ability, and character.

While communication involves the use of words, it also includes what you "don't say." *Nonverbal communication* skills include eye contact, body position-ing, appropriate touch, and both dress and appearance. *Eye contact* is a mas-sive means of communication for social workers and reveals much about your clients' emotional state and their reactions to the interventions you practice. *Body positioning* can communicate different messages to your clients. Facing the client suggests openness and safety, for example, while leaning indicates atten-tion and interest. Offering your client an *appropriate touch* is a powerful com-municative skill that can convey reassurance and understanding. Lastly, *dress and appearance* are essential nonverbal communication because the style of your clothing (formal professional or casual professional) sends a message about who you are and displays your membership in a social group or subculture. (Sheafor & Horejsi, 2012).

PRACTICE PROFESSIONAL BEHAVIORS AND ASSESS OUTCOMES

This section will help further your understanding of the practice behaviors for the 2008 CSWE EPAS 2.1.3 *Apply critical thinking to inform and communicate professional judgments*: (1) distinguish, appraise, and integrate multiple sources of knowledge, including research-based knowledge, and practice wisdom; (2) analyze models of assessment, prevention, intervention, and evaluation; and (3) demonstrate effective oral and written communication in working with individuals, families, groups, organizations, communities, and colleagues. Each question will test your application of the practice behaviors and your ability to critically think regarding their function. The questions are deliberately varied and randomly placed regarding the three critical thinking practice behaviors.

Multiple Choice

(Note: On the lines below each multiple choice question, explain why you chose that particular answer.)

Difficulty Scale: ✻ = Easy   ✻ ✻ = Moderate   ✻ ✻ ✻ = Challenging

1. Jimmy, a second year MSW student, is interning at ACME Counseling Agency and is being directly supervised by Walker, the director of social services. Walker recently received his license as a LMSW and is known for his good work in the community; however, he also has a reputation for being somewhat self-absorbed, arrogant, and at times narcissistic and prefers to mold his supervisees in his own way—to be like himself. If Jimmy has problems working under Walker, which of the following would be best for him to do?

   a. Have peer consultations with his cohorts to obtain professional growth and contact his MSW field liaison when problems arise with Walker's supervisory style.
   b. Request a meeting with ACME's agency director to discuss any problems he might have with Walker.
   c. Go along with anything that Walker does, out of respect for the fact that he is an LMSW and has his own supervisory style.
   d. Request a meeting with Walker to discuss any problems he might have with him.

   Difficulty: ✻ ✻ = Moderate
   Topic: Effective oral and written communication
   Practice Behavior: Demonstrate effective oral and written communication in working with individuals, organizations, communities, and colleagues

   _____

   _____

2. Byron is a new child welfare worker at the local welfare agency in your county. Paul, the father of three-year-old Desmond and six-year-old Efren, is voluntarily admitted into a treatment center for meth addiction, and his boys are placed in foster care. Their mother left the family when Efren was two-years-old. The foster parents contact Byron and inform him that Efren is beginning to act out. Which of the following is the best intervention for Bryon, the social worker, to do first?

   a. Discipline Efren for his acting-out behavior.
   b. Arrange for Desmond and Efren to have regular visits with their father, Paul.
   c. Enroll the foster parents in parenting classes to help them better deal with Efren's behavior and not contact Byron with every concern.

d. Move both Desmond and Efren to another foster home.

Difficulty: ✰✰ = Moderate
Topic: Intervention models
Practice Behavior: Analyze models of assessment, prevention, intervention, and evaluation

_____

_____

3. Nicole, a recent MSW graduate from one of the most reputable social work programs in the world, is owner and director of "I Care Counseling" (ICC) and is in private practice as a general practitioner. Nicole as a social worker and her private practice, ICC, are accountable in which of the following ways?

   a. Peer review by LCSWs from local social service agencies.
   b. Supervision by a diplomate in clinical social work.
   c. Continued work with a consultant who offers recommendations.
   d. Adherence to NASW Code of Ethics.

Difficulty: ✰ = Easy
Topic: Multiple sources of knowledge
Practice Behavior: Distinguish, appraise, and integrate multiple sources of knowledge, including research-based knowledge, and practice wisdom

_____

_____

4. Myron is a last semester advanced level MSW student interning at Munizzi Counseling Center. He is in his office providing marital counseling and receives the following text from the front office: "Sorry to bother you. Emergency call and he will only speak to you. Must transfer call to you. Please pick up!" Myron answers the transferred call and it is William, another one of his clients, who has a history of suicide attempts. William is crying uncontrollably and says he is thinking of committing suicide. Myron should:

   a. Tell William that he is in an appointment and that William needs to set up an appointment as soon as possible with Myron.
   b. Keep William on the phone and ask the couple to wait for him in the waiting area.
   c. Transfer William to a clinical psychologist to test for suicide potential.

d. Refer William to an inpatient psychiatric facility.

Difficulty: ✡ ✡ ✡ = Challenging
Topic: Demonstrate effective oral communication and practice wisdom
Practice Behavior: Demonstrate effective oral and written communication in working with individuals and distinguish, appraise, and integrate multiple sources of knowledge and practice wisdom

_____

_____

5. Lilly and her fourteen-year-old daughter Millie come to your office because of Millie's inappropriate sexual behavior at school and her allegation that she has been incestuous with her father, who is currently not residing in the family home. Lilly's desire is to reunite the family because of the lifestyle changes that the separation has created. What should the social worker do first?

   a. Critically think and analyze the content of Millie's allegation for authenticity and call in the father for a family session.
   b. Interview Lilly, Millie, and all the women and girls in the family for possible patterns of behavior by the father.
   c. Evaluate both the mother and daughter separately in an attempt to examine the person-in-environment with a concentration on assisting both clients in solving and preventing problems.
   d. Send a signed release of information to the original authorities in the case to obtain more data.

Difficulty: ✡ ✡ ✡ = Challenging
Topic: Intervention and evaluation
Practice Behavior: Analyze models of assessment, prevention, intervention, and evaluation

_____

_____

6. You are a LMSW at a local counseling center in your town. You obtain verbal permission from Lilly and the approval of Millie to record a portion of the family session on your smartphone. You also have the family's written permission to use the tape in supervision. You later remember that you want to download the session and use it in a presentation at the next Council on Social Work Education (CSWE) Annual Program Meeting (APM), which is a national professional conference for social workers. No such release was obtained. You ask your supervisor what to do but cannot reach her, so you text your question. You then use it at the CSWE APM, so therefore:

a. You alone bear the responsibility.
b. You and your supervisor share responsibility for the decision because you did text her and she is usually good about responding to your texts.
c. You are well within your rights to use it because you have signed permission from the family.
d. You are well within your rights to use the recording of the session at the professional conference because it will be shown only to a professional audience, most of whom are licensed experienced clinicians.

Difficulty: ✹ ✹ = Moderate
Topic: Communication with families
Practice Behavior: Demonstrate effective oral and written communication with families

_____

_____

7. Julia is a social worker at an agency that provides wraparound services to the court system in your county for juveniles dealing with anger management issues. She is having problems with her client Timothy, who is a sixteen-year-old habitual repeater. She is finding that she is becoming uncomfortably angry with Timothy and is finding it difficult to control herself. She should:

a. Consult her supervisor or consultant.
b. Go into therapy for her anger management.
c. Refer the client to someone else, because how can she counsel Timothy about his anger if she cannot control hers?
d. Hide her anger from Timothy and pretend that it is not happening.

Difficulty: ✹ ✹ ✹ = Challenging
Topic: Integrate multiple sources of knowledge
Practice Behavior: Distinguish, appraise, and integrate multiple sources of knowledge

_____

_____

8. Fran is in the first semester of her advanced year as a school social work intern at Nichols County Middle School. Johnson, the school social worker, is at another location when the school police officer brings Lois, an eleven-year-old female, into the office with serious bruises across her body. According to the school's policy, only a police officer

is authorized to take the child for medical care. The officer refuses. Fran should first:

a. Take Lois herself because she is bound by the NASW Code of Ethics to protect children.
b. Call the police officer's supervisor.
c. Ask the school administrators to become involved.
d. Call supervisor Johnson or her university liaison regarding her dilemma.

Difficulty: ✦✦ = Moderate
Topic: Communication with families
Practice Behavior: Demonstrate effective oral and written communication with individuals

---

---

9. Denise is a medical social work intern at Smithford County Hospital. Her client Harold is dying and his doctor does not wish to tell him that he is terminally ill. Denise should:

a. Respect the doctor's wishes and say nothing.
b. Share with Harold his rights to know his medical condition—and tell him honestly about his condition.
c. Tell the patient's family of his condition.
d. Talk to the doctor and offer her your or the team's help in the case.

Difficulty: ✦ = Easy
Topic: Communication
Practice Behavior: Demonstrate effective oral and written communication with individuals

---

---

10. Keyon is a clinical therapist at McGhee's Counseling Agency. George, a child, is having problems in school. One of the conditions at home is that the paternal grandmother, Martha, usurps the mother's authority. The husband, Richard, agrees with his wife, Anna, but won't deal with his mother, Martha. They all agree to counseling with Keyon. Which would be the best approach for Keyon to take with this family?

a. Work with Martha, Anna, and George.
b. Teach the paternal grandmother, Martha, to be more submissive, compliant, or even docile.

c. Teach the husband, George, assertiveness skills.

d. Work with the mother, Anna, her husband, Richard, and their child, George.

Difficulty: ✧✧ = Moderate

Topic: Assessment and intervention

Practice Behavior: Analyze models of assessment, prevention, intervention, and evaluation

---
---

11. Nooshin, a clinical social work student at David's Counseling, has had a client, Chris, in individual therapy for drug addiction for the last eighteen months. Chris has recently lost his job and raised the issue of termination of therapy due possibly to financial problems and his inability to pay for service. Nooshin should first:

    a. Discuss with Chris why he raised the issue.
    b. Speak with her supervisor, Kevin, as soon as possible.
    c. Assess if he can make further progress if the therapy is discontinued.
    d. Ask Chris if he would prefer another worker.

Difficulty: ✧ = Easy

Topic: Practice wisdom

Practice Behavior: Distinguish, appraise, and integrate multiple sources of knowledge, including practice wisdom

---
---

12. Debbie brings her five-year-old daughter, Kayla, to a social worker for evaluation. Kayla has an imaginary playmate named Ebony, who tells her to hit children who look differently than she does. The social worker should first:

    a. Do play therapy with Kayla in an effort to understand why Ebony is telling her to act out.
    b. Refer Debbie to a parent education class to better cope with and understand Kayla's behavior and Ebony's actions.

c. Explain to Debbie that Kayla's behavior is normal and should not be an area of concern.

d. Refer to a Kayla to child psychologist.

Difficulty: ✿✿ = Moderate

Topic: Intervention and evaluation

Practice Behavior: Analyze models of assessment, prevention, intervention, and evaluation

_____

_____

13. You are social worker at a chemical dependency unit. You are working with a cocaine abuser who says his father has died. He needs a pass to attend his father's funeral. The first thing you do is:

a. Refuse permission for him to attend.

b. Make a contract with him that he will not use cocaine when on a pass.

c. Check on the death of his father.

d. Allow him to go accompanied by a social worker aide.

Difficulty: ✿✿ = Moderate

Topic: Practice wisdom

Practice Behavior: Distinguish, appraise, and integrate multiple sources of knowledge, including research-based knowledge and practice wisdom

_____

_____

14. Terence is an LMSW at "Come As You Are" counseling center. Joseph and Elizabeth, a couple, are being seen in therapy for marital issues. Elizabeth has stopped working, says she's depressed, appears very stressed, states she cannot sleep, and is not eating appropriately. Throughout most of the session, Elizabeth cries uncontrollably. She complains about not being made felt important by Joseph and that she needs a major change in her life, or else. Terence should first:

a. Schedule an individual appointment with Elizabeth.

b. Suggest couples therapy.

c. Assess Elizabeth for suicide risk.

d. Refer both Joseph and Elizabeth to a psychiatrist.

Difficulty: ✵ ✵ = Moderate

Topic: Evaluation and practice wisdom

Practice Behavior: Distinguish, appraise, and integrate multiple sources of knowledge, including research-based knowledge and practice wisdom

_____

_____

15. Alonzo is in his junior year at a small state school. His maternal grandmother, Suzie, with whom he had a warm relationship, is accidently killed by police when the local police raided the wrong house looking for drugs. You, as a social worker assigned to work with members of her family, would recommend that Alonzo:

a. Be informed immediately.

b. Be informed after his exams are over.

c. Not be informed until summer vacation.

d. Be made to come home.

Difficulty: ✵ ✵ ✵ = Challenging

Topic: Communication with families

Practice Behavior: Demonstrate effective oral and written communication in working with individuals, families, groups, organizations, communities, and colleagues

_____

_____

Essay Questions

1. Discuss the application of no fewer than five of the fifteen skills and knowledge components of the critical thinking process and explain how they relate to your everyday life as advanced or second year students in your perspective MSW programs.

2. Discuss and identify at least three ways in which applying critical thinking strategies informs and communicates professional judgment as advanced or second year students in your perspective MSW programs.

3. Identify and discuss three of the four ways by which to distinguish multiple sources of knowledge for social functioning for social workers as an advanced or second year student.

4. Discuss and identify the ways in which knowledge can be assessed and integrated based on the levels of professional social work practice.

5. What is *practice wisdom*, and how do you go about appraising the multiple sources of it as advanced or second year students in your field agencies with your clients? In your answer, provide an example in which you witnessed or utilized practice wisdom.

6. Discuss the significance of critical thinking relative to analyzing models of assessment and prevention.

Role-Play Exercise: What Do I Do? How Do I Think? It Is Critical!

Actions and responses to the role-play will vary and depends on your individual characteristics, personal experience and professional knowledge, and they are from your own perspective. Learn and enjoy!

You are in your second week of your first semester of your advanced or second year MSW program and have not been placed in an agency setting. Your MSW program is relatively new and is experiencing growing pains that, up to now, had little to no effect on you. The policy regarding workplace internships is ambiguous, and you have recently secured employment at an agency where you intern and were told that you cannot intern there, but two of your cohorts are currently at a worksite internship, one who was placed at the beginning of the semester, and one who has been at the agency since the summer.

This role-play exercise can take place in either a professional formal setting or a relaxed casual setting. The minimum number of participants is four: (1) the student seeking the placement, (2) the student that currently has the worksite placement, (3) the student who has been at an agency since the summer, and (4) the field placement coordinator.

Practice with MySocialWorkLab

Visit **MySocialWorkLab** at www.mysocialworklab.com to watch these competency-based videos.

Watch

Critical Thinking—**Applying Critical Thinking**

Critical Thinking—**Demonstrating Effective Oral and Written Communication**

References

Gambrill, E., & Gibbs, L. (2009). *Critical thinking for helping professionals: A skills-based workbook*. 3rd ed. Hoboken, NJ: Oxford University Press.

Groundwater-Smith, S., & Sachs, J. (2002). The activist professional and the reinstatement of trust. *Cambridge Journal of Education, 32*(3), 341–358.

Morales, A. T., Sheafor, B. W., & Scott, M. E. (2012). *Social work: A profession of many faces* (Updated 12th ed.). Boston: Pearson Education\Allyn & Bacon.

National Association of Social Workers (1981). *Standards for the classification of social work practice, Policy Statement 4.* Silver Springs, MD: National Association of Social Workers.

O'Hare, T. (2009). *Essential skills of social work practice: Assessment, intervention, and evaluation.* Chicago: Lyceum Books.

Sheafor, B. W., & Horejsi, C. J. (2012). Techniques and guidelines for social work practice (9th ed.). Boston: Pearson Education\Allyn & Bacon.

Sternberg, R. J. (Ed.) (1990). *Wisdom: Its nature, origins and development.* New York: Cambridge University Press.

4

DIVERSITY IN PRACTICE

CSWE EPAS **2.1.4** *Engage diversity and difference in practice*

Diversity in practice, the fourth core competency of the 2008 EPAS, integrates necessary knowledge, values, and skills that present a firm foundation to build upon as an advanced or second year social work student. You will learn that diversity in practice is also integral in the shaping of human experiences and vital to the formation of identity. You learned of the "browning" and "graying" of America during your foundation year in an effort to understand the various dimensions of diversity. However, during your advanced or second year, you will learn of the multiple factors and population characteristics that will contribute to a diverse practice setting, such as age, class, color, culture, disability, ethnicity, immigration status, race, and religion. You will be educated to understand the ways in which differences of personal life experiences may lead to negative life occurrences, such as (1) oppression, (2) poverty, (3) marginalization, and (4) alienation. Experiences, for some, may also lead to positive outcomes, such as privilege, power, and acclaim (EPAS, 2008).

You will further your self-awareness to eliminate the influences of personal biases and values in working with diverse groups of people. In your advanced year, you will recognize and communicate an understanding of the importance of differences in shaping life experiences. You will continue to evaluate practice and policy procedures within the context of your cultural background, as well as within the culture of your agencies to determine how they might better serve, and be more effective within, a diverse practice. During your advanced or second year, you will begin to view yourself as a learner and engage with those who work as informants. These behaviors will serve as steps to engage with diversity and differences in practice in practicums at field agencies, as well as in private agency settings, governmental organizations, and corporate institutions beyond graduation.

RECOGNIZING CULTURAL STRUCTURES AND VALUES

Cultural ideologies frequently govern the way in which we view certain situations and how we are viewed by certain populations. You will become aware of culture and its pervasive influence during your advanced or second year as you become familiarized with the nuances of your own culture and learn about other cultures. You will acquire cultural knowledge about your clients and adapt social work skills and interventions that enable you to recognize cultural structures within your personal community and that of your client base. You will learn that the way in which to identify cultural structures is to first become culturally competent. You will read many articles and books and listen to many lectures and presentations on cultural competence during your advanced or second year; however, the NASW Code of Ethics should serve as your starting point of understanding regarding cultural competence.

The NASW Cultural Competence Standards (2009) identify a number of essentials for a culturally competent social worker. One of these is to recognize a culture's strengths and its function in human behavior and society. Another critical ability for a culturally competent social worker is to demonstrate competence in the delivery of client services that reflect an understanding and appreciation of diversity. Although problematic at times, and difficult to define, culture has the power to shape your thoughts and guide your behavior. Culture has many definitions and is not an easy concept to define but generally include norms, beliefs, customs, values, and social interpersonal relationships that govern social interaction among or between community members and outsiders (Longress, 2000).

Culture can also refer to the life patterns of a group or society and can be narrowly defined as the specific systems of meaning that we use to weigh and consider our world. Culture establishes patterns and ideas and influences our attitudes (the statements that reflect our values and beliefs) and behavior (what we do).

You will learn how to better identify your cultural values in an effort to engage diversity and difference in practice in both your classroom setting and at your field agencies as you engage in values-guided diversity in practice. You will learn during your advanced or second year that cultural values can also be seen as personal values and are the basis for ethical action. Different forms of cultural values can shape your understanding of different cultures including your *value systems*, *principle values*, and *doctrinal/ideological values*. Value systems are coherent principles of right and wrong that are adopted by individuals and are generally accepted by groups, culture, or society as standards to guide its behavior.

Principle values are the foundation upon which other values are built, and they measure integrity, while doctrinal/ideological values are religious in nature and political in structure. You will learn that some examples of values could include : openness, reputation, spirituality, cooperation, privacy, and time.

Some of the same cultural values, such as freedom, self-reliance, equality, family security, and relationships, are shared by different groups and take different priorities or significance depending on the situation. For example, in the Swedish, French, Malaysian, Japanese, Russian, and Arab cultures, clients prioritize their most important cultural values differently. The Swedish view self-reliance as a top cultural value, while people of Malaysian, Russian, and Arab cultures value family security; however, Americans and Japanese most value equality and relationships, respectively (Synergy Associates, 2011).

GAINING SELF-AWARENESS: ELIMINATING PERSONAL BIASES AND VALUES

As an advanced MSW student practitioner, you will examine in detail your attitudes and beliefs, as well as your knowledge and skills, while working with culturally different clients. You will continue your process of gaining self-awareness as you learn techniques by which to identify fundamental philosophies and master core beliefs that will allow you to engage diversity and difference in your professional practice settings. Although various definitions of self-awareness exist, it can be seen as having a clear perception of your personality, which includes your strengths, weaknesses, thoughts, beliefs, motivations, and emotions.

As you develop self-awareness, you will be able to make changes to your thought systems and the professional interpretations of situations. Self-awareness allows you to understand your clients, the way in which you believe they perceive you, your attitude, and your responses to them. Self-awareness is essential for a trained social worker; however, it is vital to your development as advanced or second year MSW students. Self-awareness is also the ability to look at and recognize not only the positive personal attributes that you bring to the profession, but also the judgmental, discriminatory, and intolerant qualities that you must acknowledge and work toward positively changing.

You will learn that you must advocate for and focus on evidence-based practice with regard to the elimination of personal biases, prejudices, and preconceived belief systems within the context of social work practice. *Beliefs* are the views and opinions that attempt to describe some aspect of your personal biases. The validity of personal biases and belief systems are not as important as the way in which those biases and beliefs shape everyday personal experiences and professional practices.

Understanding terminology will assist in eliminating personal biases based on specific characteristics of your clients such as race and ethnicity. *Race* refers to genetic differences among people that are manifested in physical characteristics such as skin color; while *ethnicity* refers to mutual group features such as physical appearance, history, religion, and culture. You will learn that ethnicity usually refers to national origin and ancestry, as reflected in the term Hispanic, and is often used in place of race to suggest that individuals in a racial group sometimes share other characteristics and experiences besides physical appearances. In eliminating personal bias from your client system, it is important that you never accept or generalize one behavior of a particular cultural group as "the" behavior of all its members.

During your advanced or second year, you will further your level of understanding regarding particular approaches to eliminating personal biases within the context of your class environment with your cohorts and professors, as well as in your practice in the field with your colleagues, agency personnel, and clients. It is important that you be aware of your personal biases; however, simple awareness is not adequate. You will learn that diversity in practice begins with the awareness that your decisions and responses to your professional behavior and that of your cohorts, professors, and those within your practice setting cannot be bias-free and neutral.

You will learn to go beyond awareness of your individual morals to address the management of your personal values and biases. You will learn many methods by which to reduce the effect of personal values and biases on your professional decisions. You will appreciate techniques for researching the cultural backgrounds of your clients, including: interacting with colleagues and cohorts who may share similar cultural characteristics; reading about the cultural background of individuals who may share the same cultural background; and inquiring about the differences among the various cultures of your client base.

RECOGNIZING, COMMUNICATING, AND UNDERSTANDING "DIFFERENCE" IN SHAPING LIFE EXPERIENCE

We all are uniquely made with obvious differences and experiences that we bring to the profession. During your advanced or second year, you will learn that recognizing the presence of apparent differences is vital to the success of engaging diversity in your practice setting. You will come to understand that differences shape your experiences and form foundations to rely upon regarding your interaction with your client base. Although you will encounter a plethora of differences, you will learn that some of the common variances that are constant with these differences are the areas of culture, race, and ethnicity, while others might concern gender identification, religion, and/or sexual orientation. Your attempts to learn about the culture and traditions of your client base will help in the trust-building process with your clients. Knowledge of and discussion regarding these differences are important, as they may communicate to your client base that you value them and appreciate their differences. Your interest also gives the client permission to talk about matters of the heart regarding these differences. Cultural values, beliefs, or customs may need to be considered when designing an intervention, developing professional relations, or delivering services.

Communicating difference in the shaping of experience is also important when engaging diversity and difference in practice. Some of the major problems that impede social workers from engaging diversity and difference arise from their inability to communicate differences in the shaping of experiences. In your perspective MSW programs, you will learn many avenues that will allow you to better communicate and appreciate differences in shaping experiences both personally with your cohorts and professors, as well as within the environment of your field-placement agencies. Acknowledging issues of racism, oppression, and discrimination, as well as inequitable policies and services adds steps to foster communication of differences that shape experience. During your advanced or second year, you will further your understanding of the importance of reflecting on your own history of prejudice, discrimination, and individual and institutional racism, and their effects on your professional attitude, perception, and behavior toward the client population you serve. You will learn that knowledge about these past and present influences can aid in your communication about differences in shaping experiences and help you successfully engage diversity and difference in practice.

As advanced or second year MSW students, you will learn the importance of understanding differences in the process of shaping experience that result in positive outcomes from your professional relationships with your clients and your excellent delivery of service to them. You will also learn that furthering your understanding in shaping experiences of your client base—by impro-ving your attitudes toward them, cultivating your belief in them, and refining your skills to assist them—will enhance outcomes of understanding differences in shaping experiences. People differ in many ways, but the most visible differences, for most, is physical appearance. You will begin to note that on some occasions and in certain situations, a client's appearance affects their life experiences, and it is important that you understand how differences such as these shape their experiences.

For example, people who are members of a racial or ethnic group are sometimes referred to as "minorities" and historically have undergone different experiences. For instance, the experiences of a deprived African American may be more similar to that of an impoverished Hispanic person than to that of a middle-class Asian. All three are members of minority racial or ethnic groups and are referred to as "minorities." In most societies, there is a majority composed of people who look "alike" in basic characteristics such as skin color; and there are minority groups of people who look "different" from the majority in terms of those characteristics. Understanding these differences is vital to engaging diversity in practice.

LEARNING AND ENGAGING WITH THOSE WHO WORK AS INFORMANTS

During your advanced or second year in your individual programs, you will further your understanding of how to work with your clients within your service delivery system. You will gain knowledge from individuals who work as informers. As you increase your self-awareness, you will gain greater flexibility and openness to the process of learning with those who work as informants. You will learn some steps by which to accomplish self-awareness and engage diversity and difference in practice would be to: (1) identify your family origins; (2) describe their disadvantages and advantages; (3) convert advantages and disadvantages; and (4) interpret findings. When you identify your family origins, you will learn the importance of identifying specific ancestors and speculating on the conditions they left behind and possible motives for leaving those conditions. This will help you describe the disadvantages and advantages your ancestors may have experienced because of their ethnicity; and look at their ethnic advantages and disadvantages (Green, 1995) to assist you in engaging with those who work as informants.

Oftentimes you will have within your caseload clients who have interfaced with the criminal justice system and are mandated for treatment; you may seek to collaborate with an individual that will assist you in holding your client accountable. You will learn the art of engaging with individuals who work as informants while bridging diversity and difference in practice. Lack of knowledge about a particular community and deficiency of a skills-set to establish communication and relationships will delay the collaborative process. Consequently, engagement with informed individuals becomes both necessary and purposeful. You will learn that engaging with the informant regarding the challenged client, such as one mandated for treatment, can: help you demonstrate fairness and hold accountable the client who is manipulative; and assist you in determining the truth of a situation when you have detected the lack of truth from your client. Finally, while working with the person as the informant, you will learn the process of assessing an informant's role conception and role expectation. *Role conception* as an informant refers to the informant's belief and assumptions in terms of behavior in his or her particular role (Sheafor & Horejsi, 2012). The informant's *role expectation* proposes the presence of a set of behaviors identified as appropriate and acceptable, in which limits of acceptable, tolerated behavior are agreed upon.

PRACTICE DIVERSITY AND ASSESS OUTCOMES

This section will help further your understanding of the practice behaviors for the 2008 CSWE EPAS 2.1.4. *Engage diversity and difference in practice*: (1) recognize the extent to which a culture's structures and values may oppress, marginalize, alienate, or create or enhance privilege and power;

(2) gain sufficient self-awareness to eliminate the influence of personal biases and values in working with diverse groups; (3) recognize and communicate understanding of the importance of difference in shaping life experiences; and (4) view yourselves as learners and engage those with whom you work as informants. Each question will test your application of the practice behaviors and your ability to critically think regarding their function. The questions are deliberately varied and randomly placed regarding the four practice behaviors of diversity in practice.

Multiple Choice

(Note: On the lines below each multiple choice question, explain why you chose that particular answer.)

Difficulty Scale: ✵ = Easy   ✵ ✵ = Moderate   ✵ ✵ ✵ = Challenging

1. Miriam is a social work intern at a private agency in your city. The Wongs, a Chinese family, have been in the United States since 2008. Mr. and Mrs. Wong are very upset that their daughter Lindsey stays after school for activities and doesn't help out at their family convenience store. Also, Lindsey wears lipstick and her parents do not approve of make-up. Miriam should counsel Mr. and Mrs. Wong that they are experiencing problems with:

   a. Separation/individualization.
   b. Displacement.
   c. Loss of sense of self.
   d. Passive resistance.

   Difficulty: ✵ ✵ = Moderate

   Topic: Recognizing cultural structures

   Practice Behavior: Recognize the extent to which a culture's structures and values may oppress, marginalize, alienate, create, or enhance privilege and power

   _____

   _____

2. An elderly Malaysian man, who is a recent immigrant, requires surgery followed by six weeks in a rehabilitation facility. He is unwilling to undergo surgery if he cannot return to his family quickly. His physician fears that the rehabilitation program may not be manageable for his family and refers them to the hospital social service department. You are the social worker who receives the referral. The best strategy for addressing this problem is to:

   a. Insist that the family follow the doctor's recommendation.
   b. Help the family understand the procedures and advantages of Western medicine.
   c. Suggest that the family wait to perform the surgery to allow more time to work with him.
   d. Discuss alternatives with the physician and the family, since Malaysian cultural norms require that elderly family members are cared for at home.

   Difficulty: ✵ ✵ ✵ = Challenging

   Topic: Recognizing cultural structures and values

Practice Behavior: Recognize the extent to which a culture's structures and values may oppress, marginalize, alienate, create, or enhance privilege and power

_____

_____

3. When dealing with an African American client, a white social worker should discuss race in the initial session because:

   a. doing so will prevent transference from occurring.
   b. doing so will show the client he or she is caring.
   c. doing so will enable the client's strong feelings to surface more quickly.
   d. the issue of race may influence what the client brings up in therapy.

   Difficulty: ✿ ✿ = Moderate
   Topic: Communicating difference in shaping experience
   Practice Behavior: Recognizing, communicating, and understanding "difference" in shaping life experience

_____

_____

4. When working with gay/lesbian clients, the therapist can expect that:

   a. Despite other concerns, sex issues are more prominent.
   b. The therapist's sexual orientation will be an issue.
   c. The clients will have more issues with authority figures.
   d. Gays and lesbians to be more impaired than the population at large.

   Difficulty: ✿ ✿ = Moderate
   Topic: Eliminating personal biases
   Practice Behavior: Gaining self-awareness: eliminating personal biases and values

_____

_____

5. You are in you're the final semester of your MSW program interning at a crisis intervention center, and Chris, an interning cohort from the first year MSW program, inquires about basic social work practice skills that form the basis of multicultural sensitivity training. The best response to Chris would be:

   a. Examining countertransference.
   b. Information gathering.

c. Developing an alliance.

d. Active listening.

Difficulty: ✵ = Easy

Topic: Communicating difference in shaping experience

Practice Behavior: Recognizing, communicating, and understanding "difference" in shaping life experience

_____

_____

6. A Haitian adolescent is in conflict with her family and culture over her American ways. She wants to date, have friends, dress like others, and go to parties. She feels very guilty. One of the things that would help her most would be:

   a. A social worker who is familiar with this kind of difficulty.

   b. The support of her peers.

   c. That her parents take lessons in English.

   d. That she and her family begin family therapy.

   Difficulty: ✵ ✵ = Moderate

   Topic: Recognizing cultural structures and values

   Practice Behavior: Recognize the extent to which a culture's structures and values may oppress, marginalize, alienate, create, or enhance privilege and power

   _____

   _____

7. Kemo, a past client, comes to you and thinks that he has AIDS. He shares with you that he has been tested twice in the last two years; however, both tests were negative and he hasn't had any symptoms. The first thing for you to do is:

   a. Provide AIDS education to Kemo.

   b. Have Kemo tested at a different clinic.

   c. Discuss Kemo joining a support group.

   d. Suggest that Kemo enter therapy.

   Difficulty: ✵ ✵ = Moderate

   Topic: Engaging with those who work as informants

   Practice Behavior: Learning and engaging with those who work as informants

   _____

   _____

8. Lawrence, a gay Broadway headliner, age sixty-one, is in treatment. Recently, his singing career has not gone well and his last performance received poor reviews. To add to his anguish, his longtime partner, Nightingale, has just been diagnosed with a terminal illness and Lawrence himself is undergoing a very uncomfortable medical treatment. Lawrence is under enormous professional and personal pressure. Lawrence contemplates depicting the life of Liza Minnelli as a great tragedy and becoming famous, after which, he will die. He complains of insomnia and loss of appetite since he returned home from a hospital stay. He has missed a number of auditions and has lost some enthusiasm for his career after discovering that his partner is seriously ill. The first thing the worker should do is:

   a. Address the unreality of Lawrence's intentions.
   b. Discuss Lawrence's feelings about his partner's illness and the possibility of his dying.
   c. Address Lawrence's feelings about returning to treatment.
   d. Address Lawrence's gender confusion.

   Difficulty: ✡ ✡ ✡ = Challenging
   Topic: Understanding differences in shaping experience
   Practice Behavior: Recognizing, communicating, and understanding "difference" in shaping life experience

   _____

   _____

9. Abdullah and Tamir are sixteen-year-old twins who immigrated to the United States from Arabia with their family three years ago. Their mother is Arabian and the father is a Somalian citizen who works as a taxi driver. The parents are discussing returning to Arabia where the children were born and spent most of their lives. The twins are deeply unhappy about returning, and Abdullah has threatened to run away if the family tries to go back to their native country. Abdullah tells the social worker that he was forced out of his public school at the age of twelve and isolated from other children because he is not considered an Arabian citizen, as his father is Somalian. His sister also does not want to go back to Arabia, but she will reluctantly comply if her parents insist. Both children are academically talented and say they would like to go to college. The social worker's best strategy is to:

   a. Reassure Abdullah and Tamir that they will simply be returning to their extended families and to their old lives.
   b. Understand the children's reaction as a normal adolescent rebellion and work with the twins to accept the family's decision.

c. Probe further to verify Abdullah's objections about returning to Arabia. If they are accurate, assist him to the extent feasible.

d. Emphasize to Abdullah and Tamir that since they have lived most of their lives in Arabia, they are still Arabian and their residence in the United States for a brief period will not affect them.

Difficulty: ✿✿✿ = Challenging

Topic: Recognizing cultural structures and values

Practice Behavior: Recognize the extent to which a culture's structures and values may oppress, marginalize, alienate, create, or enhance privilege and power

_____

_____

10. Violeta, a twenty-one-year-old, emigrated from Romania a few years ago with her family. She is involved with a mental health agency and has been diagnosed with bipolar disorder and functions quite well on medications. In the past few years, Violeta has been able to attend college as well as work part-time. However, occasionally, she refuses to take her medications, causing her mood, behavior, and attitude to change drastically. When Violeta is non-compliant, she disappears for a few days, and cuts her classes, and she refuses to discuss her activities while out of touch with her family. Her parents, Vlad and Ioana, are worried about her safety during these periods believing that she is using drugs and alcohol and behaving irresponsibly. They ask you to help the family obtain a court order to restrain their daughter's behavior. How can you first assist the family?

a. Help Vlad and Ioana find an attorney experienced in helping families of children with mental illness.

b. Ask Vlad and Ioana to bring Violeta into the agency for evaluation.

c. Help Vlad and Ioana understand the limits of the court system and work to develop strategies through which they can help Violeta continue her medications consistently.

d. Reassure the family that with a diagnosis of bipolar disorder, Violeta is unlikely to do anything destructive.

Difficulty: ✿✿✿ = Challenging

Topic: Engaging with those who work as informants

Practice Behavior: Learning and engaging with those who work as informants

_____

_____

11. William, a fifty-eight-year-old male, is referred by a health maintenance organization (HMO) primary-care doctor to mental health services for assessment. It is observed that the information about William is incomplete and doesn't indicate the specific reasons for the referral. Interviewed by a young female social worker, William seems fairly open but says he wants a clinician who is male and closer to his own age. William reveals that he has emotional and physical problems that he wants to discuss but does not feel comfortable doing so with a young woman. Though the social worker and the client talk politely for some time, he continues to insist that he is uncomfortable and will not discuss his problems with her. How should the social worker proceed?

   a. She should gently reassure William of the confidentiality of the relationship and that she is fully capable of helping him with his problem, no matter how difficult or embarrassing.

   b. Since the referral was made to her, she should notify the client that arranging another referral will be time-consuming and that he may have to wait quite a while for a new worker.

   c. She should accept the client's statements, since they have been repeated and he seems reluctant to talk with her. She should then let William know that she will honor his request and arrange for a social worker closer to his preference.

   d. William is probably masking his problems and is not amenable to treatment. No further effort should be made on his behalf.

   Difficulty: ✲✲✲ = Challenging
   Topic: Recognizing difference in shaping experience
   Practice Behavior: Recognizing, communicating, and understanding "difference" in shaping life experience

   _____

   _____

12. Angela, an MSW intern, is assigned an intake with Mathis Judge, an elderly client. Mr. Judge seems friendly, so Angela uses his first name when talking with him. During portions of the interview, Angela notices that Mathis appears reluctant and hesitant when responding to some of her questions. He withdraws further as the interview progresses. Finally, Mathis calmly tells Angela that he would prefer help from someone who is similar in age and experience to him, and that he finds her disrespectful and overly familiar. How should Angela assess this situation?

   a. That Mathis is a demanding client and should be appeased.

   b. That Mathis has an attitude problem.

    c. That Mathis is overly sensitive and may resent having to ask for service.

    d. That she misunderstood Mathis's needs and became overly informal.

Difficulty: ✿✿ = Moderate

Topic: Understanding differences in shaping experience

Practice Behavior: Recognizing, communicating, and understanding "difference" in shaping life experience

_____

_____

13. You are an LMSW at private counseling agency for substance abuse and discover that one of your female clients, Teresa, is HIV infected and is also sexually active. Teresa refuses to inform her partners of her illness and maintains that she always uses safe-sex techniques and would never knowingly put her partner at risk. You are concerned that despite Teresa's precautions, she should notify her partners. The best option for you to take is to:

    a. Do nothing.

    b. Contact the Department of Public Health and ask them to meet with Teresa.

    c. Discuss the matter fully with Teresa and explore the meaning of her behavior and the risks she is taking.

    d. Demand that Teresa stop behaving in a way that puts others at risk.

Difficulty: ✿✿✿ = Challenging

Topic: Engaging with those who work as informants

Practice Behavior: Learning and engaging with those whom work as informants

_____

_____

14. Winston, a Jamaican immigrant, receives a notice to appear at the office of the U.S. Citizenship and Immigration Services (USCIS). Fearful of government authority because of his experience in Jamaica, Winston reveals to the social worker that he lied on his immigration application and that if the lie is discovered, he might face prosecution or deportation. The social worker's first responsibility is to:

    a. Convince the client to tell the truth.

    b. Continue to provide services.

    c. Call the USCIS and inform them of the lie.

    d. Discuss Winston's concerns about alternatives that he might pursue, such as employing a lawyer.

Difficulty: ✿✿ = Moderate

Topic: Recognizing cultural structures and values

_____

_____

15. Magdalena, a supervisor at the Regional Youth Detention Center (RYDC) in you county, conducts early-morning daily prayer meetings in her office for staff interested in attending. Magdalena is an Evangelical Christian, and while she does not require attendance at her daily morning prayer meetings, it seems to staff that she shows special treatment to those who regularly attend; however, there is no evidence that staffing decisions, promotions, or recommendations are influenced by anyone's religious observance. On at least three occasions, Magdalena has sent emails to the office staff inviting anyone to attend who wishes. You feel uncomfortable about the repeated emails and interpret them as a gentle form of intimidation. The next best action for you to take is to:

   a. Discuss your concerns with Magdalena.
   b. Do nothing, as there is no evidence of favoritism.
   c. Discuss your concerns with the director of human resources.
   d. Discuss the matter with county officials.

   Difficulty: ✵ ✵ = Moderate
   Topic: Gaining self-awareness: eliminating personal biases and values
   Practice Behavior: Gain sufficient self-awareness to eliminate the influence of personal biases and values in working with diverse groups

_____

_____

16. Alexandra is a recent MSW graduate from CAU, a Historical Black College and University (HBCU) in a large metropolitan city. She considers herself to be a culturally competent practitioner; however, she is confronted by a client of an ethnic, racial, and social group unfamiliar to her. The next most appropriate action for Alexandra to take is to:

   a. Transfer the client to someone more knowledgeable.
   b. Expect the client to teach her about the culture.
   c. Actively seek knowledge.
   d. Change nothing, as these differences are irrelevant with skillful interviewing.

   Difficulty: ✵ = Easy
   Topic: Gaining self-awareness: eliminating personal biases and values

Practice Behavior: Gain sufficient self-awareness to eliminate the influence of personal biases and values in working with diverse groups

_____

_____

17. You are a social worker in private practice, and one of your regular clients, Frederick, comes into your office upset and disappointed at not being called back after a job interview. He vents his anger at the job interviewer. At his counseling session, your best response is:

   a. "I understand how you feel about this. These are hard times, and everyone needs a job."
   b. "I can see you're upset about this."
   c. "You have to be patient in a job search and keep looking."
   d. "I guess you're hurt and angry about not getting the job."

   Difficulty: ✷ = Easy
   Topic: Communicating difference in shaping experience
   Practice Behavior: Recognizing, communicating, and understanding "difference" in shaping life experience

_____

_____

18. Sarah Sue, a white teenage mother, is referred to Lillie May, an older African American social worker at Families Always, a community-based family agency. Lillie May might initially:

   a. Refer Sarah Sue to another social worker with similar characteristics.
   b. Recommend that Sarah Sue tell her about how the agency and the social worker can help.
   c. Talk about their differences.
   d. Note that she has worked with many young women with children.

   Difficulty: ✷ = Easy
   Topic: Learning with those who work as informants
   Practice Behavior: Learning and engaging with those who work as informants

_____

_____

19. Xavier is a social work intern in his second or advanced year, placed at a local community services board. The agency seeks to match clients with social workers according to ethnic identity and language proficiency. Xavier, in his efforts to follow the procedures of the community services board, is demonstrating:

   a. Due diligence.
   b. Affirmative action.
   c. Compliance with Title 7A of the Employment Act of 1983.
   d. Cultural sensitivity.

Difficulty: ✶ = Easy
Topic: Eliminating personal biases
Practice Behavior: Gaining self-awareness: eliminating personal biases and values

_____

_____

20. Julia, a neighbor in your subdivision, comes to your office and admits that her husband, Robert, has been beating her for several years, but she is afraid to report the violence and reluctant to leave him. Twice, the police have responded to neighbors' complaints and arrested Robert, but the abuse stops only for a short time. As her social worker, you might first consider:

   a. Helping Julia understand that she has options and work with her to explore moving to a protected women's shelter, if she is willing.
   b. Assessing the reasons (both conscious and unconscious) that might contribute to keeping Julia in an abusive marriage and provide information about resources, should she choose to make a change.
   c. Referring Julia to a battered women's group, allowing her to identify with other women in similar situations.
   d. Requesting that the agency attorney discuss Julia's legal rights with her.

Difficulty: ✶ ✶ = Moderate
Topic: Engaging with those who work as informants
Practice Behavior: Learning and engaging with those who work as informants

_____

_____

Essay Questions

1. Discuss how your understanding of cultural ideologies assists you in viewing situations within the context of your client base and helps you adapt social work skills and interventions in your practicums.

2. Identify and discuss two forms of cultural values and explain how an understanding of them assists in shaping your personal values and ethical actions. Provide an example to support your answer.

3. Define *self-awareness* and discuss some traits that exist as you begin the process of recognizing personal attributes that you bring to the profession that both help and possibly hinder your relationship with your clients and your service delivery to them.

4. Identify two key concepts or terms that are important to recognize in your attempt to eliminate personal biases and engage diversity and differences in practice.

5. Discuss the importance of recognizing and communicating differences in shaping experiences that result in diversity in practice.

6. Discuss the correlation between the importance of understanding differences in shaping experience and the delivery of excellent service to your client system.

7. Discuss several situations in which you have encountered or observed personal appearance and/or physical characteristics dictating the quality of service delivery.

8. Identify and discuss two steps that will help you engage with those who work as informants in diversity and difference in practice.

Role-Play Exercise: Diverse or Different, That Is the Question

Actions and responses to the role-play will vary and depend on your individual characteristics, personal experience, and professional knowledge and are from your own perspective. Learn and enjoy!

Share and then role-play the details of a case from your practicum experience in the agency setting at your field placement. The case must be one that, at the time you observed it, seemed to present special difficulties in terms of (1) cross-cultural communication, (2) agreement on the nature of the problem or compliance with treatment plans, and (3) the factors of racial, religious, or cultural differences. Recall what was said and who did what. Then critique the case.

Each participant must role-play their response to any of the three different scenarios of how they would go about responding to the dilemma in terms of *engaging diversity and difference in practice*.

This role-play exercise can take place in either a professional setting, such as in the waiting area of the agency, or a relaxed, casual setting such as in a coffee shop. The minimum number of participants is four: (1) the student regarding the cross-cultural communication and (2) a student regarding an agreement on the nature of the problem or compliance with treatment plans.

Practice with MySocialWorkLab

Visit **MySocialWorkLab** at www.mysocialworklab.com to watch these competency-based videos.

Watch

Diversity in Practice—**Building Self-Awareness**

Diversity in Practice—**Engaging the Client to Share Their Experiences of Alienation, Marginalization, and/or Oppression**

Diversity in Practice—**Learning From the Client to Co-create an Action Plan**

References

Council on Social Work Education (CSWE). (2008). Educational policy and accreditation standards. Retrieved April 23, 2011, from *http://www.cswe. org/Accreditaton/Handbook*

Green, J. W. (1995). *Cultural awareness in the human services: A multi-ethnic approach* (2nd ed.). Boston: Allyn & Bacon.

Longress, J. F. (2000). *Human behavior in the social environment* (3rd ed.). Itasca, IL: F. E. Peacock.

National Association of Social Workers. (2009). Cultural competence in the social work profession. In *Social Work Speaks: NASW Policy Statements*. Washington, DC: NASW Press.

Sheafor, B. W., & Horejsi, C. J. (2012). Techniques and guidelines for social work practice (9th ed.). Boston: Pearson Education/Allyn & Bacon.

Synergy Associates, Inc. (2011). Cultural values overview. Retrieved May 23, 2011, from *http://www.synergy-associates.com/cultural/corner.htm#publications*

5

HUMAN RIGHTS AND JUSTICE

CSWE EPAS 2.1.5 *Advance human rights and social and economic justice*

Human rights and justice is the fifth core competency of the 2008 EPAS and incorporates necessary knowledge, values, and skills that unequivocally present a firm foundation to build upon in order to advance civil liberties and social economic justice for your clients as an advanced or second year social work student. You will learn that your knowledge of human rights about freedom, safety, privacy, adequate standard of living, health care, and education, as well as understanding the concept of justice, are fundamental to ensuring equitable treatment for your clients.

You will begin to recognize the interconnectedness of oppression as you increase your knowledge of the various theories of justice and learn and adopt the different methods by which to advance human and civil rights.

As advanced or second year MSW students, you will learn to integrate social justice practice within the platform of your practicum experiences as you work to ensure that the basic human rights of your clients are fairly adhered to without prejudice. You will also develop an innovative understanding of how to advance human rights and social and economic justice by furthering your understanding of the forms and mechanisms of oppression and discrimination. You will also learn methods by which to advocate for human rights and social and economic justice; and you will learn steps to engage in practices that advance the social and economic justice of your client base (EPAS, 2008). Finally, you will gain knowledge of implementation strategies for advancing human rights and social and economic justice based on an understanding of forms and mechanisms of oppression and discrimination that possibly operate within environments of your perspective practicum setting.

UNDERSTANDING FORMS AND MECHANISMS OF OPPRESSION AND DISCRIMINATION

You studied the concepts of oppression and discrimination during your foundation policy course and discussed them in your practice and research courses at your perspective MSW programs. However, during your advanced or second year studies, you will further your knowledge of oppression by distinguishing among the various forms and mechanism of oppression, particular for disenfranchised groups within the United States. In your foundation policy course, you learned that the concept of oppression involved placing extreme limitations and constraints on people in groups or large systems and that oppression can occur because of structural inequalities within a society (Nichols, 2012).

Though quite indirect at times, oppression is mediated by many elements within a complex social system. Many of your clients will experience varying degrees of oppression, depending upon their social location or place in life; however, in the context of human rights and social justice, oppression occurs when people are pushed down by societies.

The oppression that you will possibly witness will be the result of social forces that hold your clients down and block their abilities and those of their families or social groups from leading good and productive lives. There are many forms of oppression that you will learn about as advanced or second year MSW students, including racism, sexism, and ageism. You will learn that *racism* can be seen as a social pattern in which people who are identified as members of a specific racial group are treated differently from people who are members of anther racial group. *Sexism* is an attitude or behavior based on traditional stereotypes of sexual roles that are discriminatory and devaluating simply based on a person's sex. *Ageism* is a social pattern in which people of a certain chronological age are treated differently, to an unnecessary degree, than those who are not of the same age group, such as in the delivery of services or in pursuit of employment.

During your second or advanced year, you will learn that the mechanism of oppression can take on many forms, some of which can be categorized in the following areas: external, internalized, and horizontal/hostility oppression (Anderson & Middleton, 2005; Gil, 1998). External oppression occurs when an individual, family, or groups with power harms an other individual, family, or group. It can occur when an oppressed client or client group gives into and becomes exactly what the oppressor's message communicated would happen. This mechanism of oppression is often accompanied by the individual or group exhibiting (1) low self-worth, (2) low self-esteem, (3) loneliness, and (4) despair (DuBois & Miley, 2011). Internalized oppression is internalizing negative judgments of being "the other," leading to self-hatred, depression, despair, and self-abuse. Horizontal or hostility oppression, on the other hand, is extended internalized oppression within one's entire group as well as toward other subordinate groups, rather than toward members of dominant groups (Anderson & Middleton, 2005; Gil, 1998). This mechanism of oppression can occur when oppressed clients or client groups take their repressed anger out on other oppressed clients or client groups either within or across oppressed groups, such as in black-on-black crime.

During your advanced or second year, you will continue to evolve your understanding of the various forms of discrimination and further learn the mechanisms by which they can be carried out. You will learn that the concept of discrimination has many definitions and that discrimination can take on many forms relative to your client base. Discrimination can be seen as negatively and/or unfairly treating an individual, family, or group based on preconceived notions about them. This negative treatment can focus on any population; however, in the case of your client base, it could include negatively making a distinction because of age, ethnicity, culture, class, religion, and physical or mental disability and according to such groups as "people of color, women, and gay and lesbian persons" (CSWE, 2008).

As advanced or second year MSW student advocate, you will learn that discrimination is not simply a belief or attitude; conversely, it is the expression of those beliefs and attitudes through a particular behavior, action, treatment, or outcome. Discrimination includes any distinction, exclusion, limitation, or preference that, being based on race, color, sex, language, religion, political or other opinion, national or social origin, economic condition or birth, has the intention or outcome of eradicating or impairing equality of treatment for your client base (Gil, 1998). You will discover that just as there are many definitions of discrimination, there are also various understandings of the forms of discrimination, which you will learn of and discuss during your advanced or second year of your MSW program. Some of the common forms of discrimination that you must come to understand include racial and religious discrimination, and discrimination based on national origin.

As advanced or second year students, you will learn that racial discrimination is inequitable or abusive behavior toward an individual, family, or group of another race because of their racial origin. In the case of your client base, it is the ability to delay, prevent, and/or decrease social benefits, services, or opportunities for someone who is eligible and or entitled, based upon race. The First Amendment to the U. S. Constitution addresses freedom of religion, press, and expression, yet religious discrimination persists. It involves treating individuals, families, groups, and/or communities unfavorably because of religious beliefs. Religious discrimination, on the other hand, has many paths but typically involves the mistreatment of an individual, family, or group because of their religious, ethical, or moral beliefs. This form of discrimination can be very subtle and can take many paths. It can be the focus of contention toward you as a student in your perspective programs and toward your client base in the field, as well.

You will learn that there are a number of understandings regarding national-origin discrimination; however, it entails the negative and disparaging treatment of individuals due solely on their ethnicity, accent, and assumed or proven country of origin. It also can involve the unfavorable treatment toward people associated with a person of a certain national origin or because of their connection with an ethnic organization or group. You will also begin to understand possible mechanisms or methods of discrimination, some of which include direct and indirect discrimination (Anderson & Middleton, 2005; Gil, 1998). Direct discrimination, as it relates to your practice, is the most obvious mechanism of discrimination. It can refer to an action that explicitly specifies the traits for which a person is being excluded or discriminated against regarding the access to goods and services (Anderson & Middleton, 2005).

During your advanced or second year, you will learn that sometimes less apparent or evident, indirect discrimination happens when discrimination occurs unintentionally in a situation that has an adverse effect on the delivery of services to an individual, family, or group based on their race, skin color, ethnicity, and other similar characteristics (Gil, 1998). Indirect discrimination can occur when some other traits that are named as being discriminated against can be reliably linked to a group vulnerable to discrimination. In order to continue providing the optimal service to your clients in your advanced or second year practicums, you must continually examine and think critically about the concepts of oppression and discrimination in your classes with your cohorts, professors, and university administrator and their significance in your own personal lives.

ADVOCATING FOR HUMAN RIGHTS AND SOCIAL AND ECONOMIC JUSTICE

You will learn to advocate for human rights as you continue to develop your understanding that both direct and indirect discrimination can be based on factors such as age, class, culture, disability, ethnicity, religion, and sexual orientation. In your efforts to advocate for human rights, you will learn that sometimes an individual practice or an agency policy appears fair, as it equally applies to the entire client base of an organization; however, upon a closer review of these practices and policies, the effect is that certain populations are being treated unfairly, making these policies unreasonable through indirect discrimination (Jimenez, 2010). As you learn to identify direct and indirect discrimination, your skills set will expand regarding your ability to advocate for the human rights of your clients.

You will learn to continue to advocate for the human rights of your clients and for social and economic justice by furthering your knowledge of the fundamental rights, privileges, opportunities, and freedoms afforded to all humans regardless of race, ethnicity, socioeconomic status, culture, national origin, religion, physical ability, sexual orientation, age, class, veteran status, political ideology, mental status, and or lifestyle (Nichols, 2012). You will also learn that as you are better able to understand the forms and mechanisms of oppression and discrimination, you will better advocate for your clients in your field placements.

ADVANCING SOCIAL AND ECONOMIC JUSTICE

In your first year of your MSW program, you learned that justice implies a set of universal principles that guide you in judging what is right and what is wrong regardless of the culture and society in which one lives. You were also introduced to several of the thirty articles of the Universal Declaration of Human Rights (UDHR) and began to understand their infusion within the foundation of the NASW Code of Ethics. Conversely, during your advanced or second year, you will learn to further your understanding of the methods by which to advance social and economic justices for your client by further delving into and securing an advanced interpretation of the Universal Declaration of Human Rights and their application to the profession. Your mastery of the NASW Code of Ethics, along with several of the key articles of the Universal Declaration of Human Rights, will assist you in advancing human rights and social and economic justice for your clients.

Some of the articles you will master during your advanced or second year include: (1) Article 1—Innate human rights; (2) Article 10—Fair and public hearing; and (3) Article 15—Right to nationality. You will learn that *innate human rights* as adopted by the UDHR espouse that everyone is born "free and equal in dignity and rights" and that people have "reason and conscience" to be treated in the "spirit of brotherhood" (United Nations, 1948). Article 10, *fair and public hearing,* suggests that every person is to have a "fair and public hearing" by a neutral and unbiased court in determining their rights and obligations relative to any criminal charge against them. You will come to appreciate an understanding of articles 1 and 10 with your clients regarding the advancement of social justice (United Nations, 1948).

Article 15, clients' *rights to nationality* states that every person has a right to nationality and should not randomly be disadvantaged of the opportunity nor deprived of the right to change his or her nationality (United Nations, 1948). These rights are engrained in the fabric of the NASW Code of Ethics and are the command for the profession in its efforts to advance social and economic justice. As second year social work students, you will continue to learn methods and techniques to adopt in your endeavors to competently advocate for human rights, social justice, and economic fairness for your clients.

PRACTICE ADVOCATING FOR HUMAN RIGHTS AND JUSTICE AND ASSESS OUTCOMES

This section will help further your understanding of the practice behaviors for the 2008 CSWE EPAS 2.1.5. *Advance human rights and social and economic justice*: (1) understanding the forms and mechanisms of oppression and discrimination; (2) advocating for human rights and social and economic justice; and (3) engaging in practices that advance social and economic justice. Each question will test your application of the practice behaviors and your ability to critically think regarding their function. The questions are deliberately varied and randomly placed regarding the three human rights and justice practice behaviors.

Multiple Choice

(Note: On the lines below each multiple choice question, explain why you chose that particular answer.)

Difficulty Scale:　✳ = Easy　　✳ ✳ = Moderate　　✳ ✳ ✳ = Challenging

1. Jermaine and Kay are advanced social work students interning in their last semester at a local advocacy agency. Jermaine has witnessed on a countless number of occasions Kay's attitude toward clients of a certain chronological age such that she subtly treats them negatively to an unnecessary degree than those who are not of the same age group, particularly in the delivery of services to them. Jermaine should:

   a. Do nothing in anticipation that Kay's discrimination will be observed by their supervisor or someone on the administrative staff at the advocacy agency.
   b. Talk to the director of the agency.
   c. First speak to Kay about her actions as to make her aware of them, and then suggest that she discuss them with the director of field education at their university and obtain some assistance.
   d. First speak to their supervisor.

   Difficulty: ✳ ✳ = Moderate
   Topic: Understanding of oppression such as ageism
   Practice Behavior: Understanding the forms and mechanisms of oppression and discrimination

   _____

   _____

2. Sahara, a Licensed Clinical Social Worker (LCSW), owns Yes We Can Help, an agency that specializes in providing services to individuals who fall victim to negative and disparaging treatment based solely on their ethnicity, accent, and/or assumed or proven country of origin. Sahara is passionate about ensuring that all clients receive the needed services for which they are eligible, particularly health services. Yes We Can Help is having difficulty attracting undocumented local Hispanic residents for services that they clearly need because many are afraid of the possibility of being reported to U. S. Citizenship and Immigration Services (USCIS), which could result in their deportation. In order to better service this population, the next best move for Sahara and the staff at Yes We Can Help is to:

   a. Start a Facebook account specifically soliciting poor Hispanic clients.
   b. Hire local trusted Hispanic residents to visit community members and do outreach to reassure the community that Yes We Can Help

maintains client confidentiality and will not reveal people's identity or immigration status.

   c. Ask the local school superintendent to have school principals refer clients to Yes We Can Help.

   d. Offer outreach medical services.

Difficulty: ✬✬✬ = Challenging

Topic: Understanding forms of discrimination such as national origin

Practice Behavior: Understanding the forms and mechanisms of oppression and discrimination

_____

_____

3. Luther, a social worker at a small local social service agency, receives a referral of an HIV-positive client who is emotionally unable to follow through on self-care requirements. Luther is a recent MSW graduate and has no experience treating clients with these characteristics and little knowledge of HIV/AIDS. Although he lacks practical experience in the area of HIV/AIDS, Luther decides to accept the referral. Which statement is most correct?

   a. Luther should test the situation and rely on his wits as necessary.

   b. The dilemma is a normal occurrence for new MSW graduates, and HIV-positive status adds little complexity for Luther to address.

   c. Luther is within his right to accept the client, but he must also accept an obligation to learn more about HIV/AIDS, in order to provide the most effective care to his client.

   d. It is a mistake and an ethical breach for Luther to accept a case for which he has inadequate qualifications.

Difficulty: ✬✬✬ = Challenging

Topic: Advancing social justice

Practice Behavior: Engaging in practices that advance social and economic justice

_____

_____

4. Hosea, a young Hispanic boy, is tested by his school's psychologist, Mr. White. Hosea's parents have experienced some unpleasant encounters with Mr. White and feel that he treats Hosea differently from other children who are members of another racial group. The testing reveals a learning problem. Hosea's parents disagree with the results. Which is the best recommendation a social worker can make for this family?

   a. Suggest tutoring to reinforce Hosea's learning.

   b. Consult another psychologist outside the school system.

c. Suggest that the school test Hosea again during the next six weeks.

d. Help Hosea's parents accept the results of the test.

Difficulty: ✿ = Easy

Topic: Understanding the forms of discrimination

Practice Behavior: Understanding the forms and mechanisms of oppression and discrimination

_____

_____

5. Deborah, a fifteen-year-old girl, is referred to the school social worker because she is daydreaming in class, is habitually absent and late, complains of a variety of infirmities because of the sins of the classroom, and completes few homework assignments because of her religious obligations. Her teacher reports that Deborah seems hyper-religious and at times overly concerned for others. After several meetings with Deborah, you ask to see both of her parents. Deborah's father declines to accept the invitation to meet, citing that "the Lord hadn't told him to meet." Deborah's mother agrees to meet but is defensive while discussing an appointment over the phone. She tells you that the responsibility for their daughter's difficulty lies with the school and that she does not feel that the school has Deborah's best interests at heart. The mother, too, is known to be generally resistant and hyper-religious. The first step you should take is to:

a. See only Deborah and her mother.

b. Refer Deborah and her family to a faith-based family agency, hoping that they can engage the family more successfully.

c. Call Deborah's father to assure him that the school shares an interest in helping Deborah's parents and encouraging him to attend.

d. Agree that it is probably better to continue seeing Deborah alone, until both parents can be convinced to come.

Difficulty: ✿ ✿ ✿ = Challenging

Topic: Understanding forms of discrimination such as religious discrimination

Practice Behavior: Understanding the forms and mechanisms of oppression and discrimination

_____

_____

6. You are a supervisor at a local community services board (CSB) and observe that some social work interns and some staff are rude, impolite, and at times subtly offensive with clients of color and appear to be insolent, aloof, and overly hasty with older clients. Concerned that these clients will view the agency negatively, you decide to take action. However, you are concerned that the problem may be structural, rather

than simply limited to a few problem employees. In designing a strategy, you, as director, are likely to achieve the best results by:

a. Working with each intern's university field director in setting up a serious of penalties and rewards for good performance.

b. Speaking with the perspective universities and establishing a broadly based committee that brings together all segments of the agency, including clients, and asking them to develop methods for assessing the problem and proposing solutions.

c. Talking directly with the interns who appear to lack cultural sensitivity.

d. Asking the school to perform a cultural assessment on each intern about whom you have concerns.

Difficulty: ✫✫ = Moderate

Topic: Advocating for human rights

Practice Behavior: Advocating for human rights and social and economic justice

_____

_____

7. Jackie, a social work supervisor in a health care social agency, learns that the agency's hiring officer has been diverting job applications from applicants of certain ages, social classes, and sexual orientation. Jackie further learns that the hiring officer has the full approval of the agency director. As a result, applicants of certain ages, social classes, and sexual orientation are never considered for employment, though they are perhaps qualified. What ethical principles drawn from the NASW Code of Ethics should guide Jackie's actions in this situation?

a. Jackie's first responsibility is to help workers manage their caseloads and learn from practice experience, and she is not responsible for every action of the agency.

b. Jackie should explore her own values and act accordingly.

c. Jackie should resign from the agency, both as a protest and because the agency is behaving unethically.

d. Jackie should take aggressive professional action to end the discrimination, possibly by following the chain of authority and reporting the unethical actions of the agency.

Difficulty: ✫✫ = Moderate

Topic: Advocating for human rights

Practice Behavior: Advocating for human rights and social and economic justice

_____

_____

8. Phil, a social work intern at a local social service agency, is conducting an ongoing group with clients at a local drug treatment agency. Jill, a member of the group, complains about her caseworker. The issue seems to involve Jill feeling that she is unintentionally being treated unfairly because of a past situation that had an adverse effect on the delivery of services to her simply because her ethnicity. Jill has also expressed feelings about not getting enough attention from the group members. Phil should:

   a. Suggest that Jill discuss the matter with her caseworker after allowing her to express her feeling with the group.
   b. Raise the issue at the next staff meeting.
   c. Speak to the caseworker in private about the matter concerning Jill.
   d. Allow Jill to express her feelings and encourage the group to help her resolve the issue.

   Difficulty: ✦✦✦ = Challenging
   Topic: Understanding mechanisms of discrimination such as indirect discrimination
   Practice Behavior: Understanding the forms and mechanisms of oppression and discrimination

   _____

   _____

9. Lorna, a seventeen-year-old bisexual female, comes to you regarding her desire to tell her parents about her sexuality. The first thing you would help Lorna do is:

   a. to enter into a relationship with someone who is comfortable with her own orientation.
   b. to acknowledge her sexual orientation to herself.
   c. to create a Facebook page for bisexual teenagers.
   d. to recognize that she can end her isolation by acknowledging her sexual preference.

   Difficulty: ✦ = Easy
   Topic: Advocating for human rights
   Practice Behavior: Advocating for human rights and social and economic justice

   _____

   _____

10. Chrysta, a community development social worker, has been asked to go into a community to ensure cooperation with the program. Chrysta should first:

   a. Consult political leaders, since people will go along with them.
   b. Advertise in local papers.

c. Go to local social gatherings and be seen around the area.

d. Set up a political base—a power base with representatives from schools, churches, businesses, and so on.

Difficulty: ✦✦ = Moderate

Topic: Advancing social justice

Practice Behavior: Engaging in practices that advance social and economic justice

_____

_____

11. Alphonso, an intern child protection service (CPS) worker at a county Department of Family and Children Services (DFCS) is working with sixteen-year-old Milton, who accuses his father of showing him inappropriate explicit sexual material. Alphonso's first action after the initial assessment would be to:

a. Help the father to explore and see the child's viewpoint.

b. Create a safety plan for Milton.

c. Get Milton out of the home.

d. See to it that the entire family has treatment.

Difficulty: ✦ = Easy

Topic: Advocating for human rights

Practice Behavior: Advocating for human rights and social and economic justice

_____

_____

12. Mr. and Mrs. Brown, a minority couple, are trying to adopt non-minority twins, Sally and Jane. Mr. Brown must secure larger housing as a term of the adoption. Mr. and Mrs. Brown share with you that they are able to obtain a mortgage from a local bank; however, they believe that their real estate agent, because of their racial makeup, has excluded specific areas of the city from consideration. As a social work intern, you should first:

a. Discuss the matter with the Browns.

b. Discuss the issue with your supervisor for guidance on what to do.

c. Notify the NASW ethics committee.

d. Report the information to the real estate company.

Difficulty: ✦ = Easy

Topic: Advocating for human rights

Practice Behavior: Advocating for human rights and social and economic justice

_____

_____

13. Jay, a seventeen-year-old college student, goes to the dentist for a cleaning and is informed by his dentist that he is HIV-infected. On the same day, he is referred to you, the social worker on duty at a local counseling agency. Jay is beside himself and verging on hysteria. He is tearful, confused, and very anxious. Jay states that he does not wish to tell his father and is unsure about whether to tell his partner. He states that he has no future and will never have sex again. You should first:

    a. Treat this moment as a crisis and help Jay to express his fears and disappointment.
    b. Reassure Jay about the course of HIV and suggest that he has many years and there may be a cure before very long.
    c. Help Jay to understand the importance of informing his partner.
    d. Explore the reasons he does not wish to tell his father.

    Difficulty: ✵ ✵ = Moderate
    Topic: Advancing social justice
    Practice Behavior: Engaging in practices that advance social and economic justice

    _____

    _____

14. The director of field education at your school learns that a field placement agency has a history of denying promotions to anyone who clearly professes religious faith. Several lawsuits against the agency have been won by the employees over the past few years, and the agency has been sanctioned by NASW. The agency has not taken any steps to correct the problem. The school should:

    a. Inform students assigned to the agency and give them an opportunity to choose another placement.
    b. Give notice to the agency that student placement arrangements will be discontinued.
    c. Advise the agency of the school's concerns.
    d. Not interfere in the agency's operations.

    Difficulty: ✵ = Easy
    Topic: Advancing social justice
    Practice Behavior: Engaging in practices that advance social and economic justice

    _____

    _____

15. You are in your final semester at your field placement and have accepted a position with the agency. You overhear an employee making derogatory and negative remarks about a Muslim client with the agency director. Your first step is to:

    a. Tell another intern what you heard.
    b. Tell the Muslim client what was said.
    c. Tell your supervisor that you overheard her.
    d. Do nothing.

    Difficulty: ✳ = Easy
    Topic: Advancing social justice
    Practice Behavior: Engaging in practices that advance social and economic justice

    _____

    _____

Essay Questions

1. Identify and discuss two forms of discrimination and provide an example of each that you have either experienced personally or witnessed professionally.

2. Identify and discuss two of three mechanisms of oppression and provide at least one example of each that you have experienced, witnessed, or heard discussed at your field placement.

3. Discus how securing a clear understanding of direct and indirect mechanisms of discrimination aids your ability to better advocate for the human the rights of your clients.

4. Identify and discuss two of the four articles of the Universal Declaration of Human Rights and provide an example of how your mastery of them aids in advancing social and economic justice for your clients.

5. Discuss ways in which you have advanced the human rights and social and economic justice of a client, colleague, or community member since your matriculation in your perspective MSW programs.

Role-Play Exercise: To Discriminate or Not to Discriminate, That Is the Question

Actions and responses to the role-play "To Discriminate or Not to Discriminate, That Is the Question" will vary and depend on your individual characteristics, personal experience, and professional knowledge and are from your own perspective. Learn and enjoy!

You are a member of an ethnic minority and interviewing for a field placement at an agency that has a reputation for accepting "good and exceptional students." However, it is well known in your community that the agency director and the majority of the agency administration feel that some minorities are "good" at practice but very few are "exceptional." A graduate from your placement, who is not an ethnic minority, shares with you that her supervisor is looking for an advanced or second year student for a paid placement with the potential of full-time employment after graduation.

Each participant must role-play how they would go about demonstrating attributes that advance the human rights and social and economic justice of each scenario or situation. You can role-play these in groups of three. The role-play exercise can take place in either a professional formal setting or a relaxed casual setting. The minimum number of role-play participants is three (1) the ethnic minority seeking the placement; (2) the MSW graduate who shares the information about the placement opportunity; and (3) the field placement coordinator at the university that you attend.

Practice with MySocialWorkLab

Visit **MySocialWorkLab** at www.mysocialworklab.com to watch these competency-based videos.

Watch

Human Rights and Justice—**Social and Economic Justice: Understanding Forms of Oppression and Discrimination**

Human Rights and Justice—**Advocating for Human Rights and Social and Economic Justice**

References

Anderson, S. K., & Middleton, V. A. (2005). *Explorations in privilege, oppression, and diversity.* Belmont, CA: Brooks Cole.

Council on Social Work Education (2008). Glossary to *Educational Policy and Accreditation Standards* developed by commission of the Council on Social Work Education. Alexandria, VA: Author.

DuBois, B., and Miley, K. K. (2011). *Social work: An empowering profession* (7th Ed.). Boston: Pearson Education/Allyn & Bacon.

Gil, D. G. (1998). *Confronting injustice and oppression.* New York: Columbia University Press.

Jimenez, J. (2010). *Social policy and social change: Toward the creation of social and economic justice.* Los Angeles, CA: Sage.

National Association of Social Workers (2006). International policy on human rights. In *Social Work Speaks, 2006–2009* (7th ed.). Washington, DC: Author.

Nichols, Q. (2012). *Connecting core competencies: A workbook for social workers.* Boston: Pearson Education/ Allyn & Bacon.

United Nations (1948). Universal declaration of human rights. Retrieved May 29, 2011, from *http://www.un.org/en/documents/udhr/index.shtml*

6

RESEARCH BASED PRACTICE

CSWE EPAS 2.1.6 *Engage in research-informed practice and practice-informed research*

Research-based practice is the sixth core competency of the 2008 EPAS and also provides a solid foundation to build upon as an advanced or second year social work student. The techniques that you will learn will allow you to utilize your practice experiences from your foundation year to inform research both in the classroom and in the field during your second year. As an MSW first year student, you began to grasp a level of foundational awareness with regard to the relationship between practice evaluation and the utilization of research skills. However, during your advanced or second year, you will learn how to employ evidence-based interventions as you evaluate your own practice and practice skills.

You will also learn to employ research findings as tools by which to improve practice and policy in the social service delivery to your client base.

As a core competency, research-based practice critical thinking seeks to improve the quality of the professional opinions, ethical decisions, and reasoned discernment for social workers. As an advanced or second year MSW student, you will grasp the relevance of qualitative and quantitative research and understand the scientific and ethical approaches to the building-knowledge process that will enable you to engage in research-informed practice and practice-informed research. You will further learn the process by which to use your practice experiences to inform scientific inquiry as well as research evidence to inform your practice.

USING EXPERIENCE TO INFORM SCIENTIFIC INQUIRY

You will learn that research begins with a gap in understanding and lack of knowledge that sparks a certain level of inquiry to fill that gap, and as advanced or second year MSW students, you will further your understanding of the steps and methods for filling those gaps.

You will utilize past experiences in practices as you learn the scientific processing skills that will enable you to critically think and organize your thoughts around practice. You will continue to learn to observe the behaviors of your clients in ways that are relevant to scientific inquiry that result in being able to engage in research-informed practice. There are a number of methods to an evidence-research-based practice that will enable you to better serve your clients with informed interventions that are successful.

You will learn that scientific inquiry can be seen as a way to examine or explore your client and propose explanations for his or her behavior.

During your advanced or second year, you will learn many fields, methods, or steps of scientific inquiry applicable to the various diverse areas and problem situations of your client base. Some of these might include: (1) posing a question, (2) developing a hypothesis, (3) designing an experiment, (4) collecting and interpreting the data, (5) drawing a conclusion, and (6) communicating your findings in your practice behavior (Rubin & Babbie, 2008). You will learn that by using your experiences to inform scientific inquiry as advanced or second year MSW students, you will be able to (1) gather in-depth understandings of your client base; (2) generate knowledge from past experiences that informs current practice; and (3) practice behaviors that result in successful interventions.

USING EVIDENCE-BASED RESEARCH TO INFORM PRACTICE

During your foundation research courses, you developed an understanding of the fundamentals of social work research becoming familiar with terms such as *hypothesis, theory, dependent/independent variables,* and *sampling.* You also grasped an understanding of the important components or mechanisms of research and the roles they play in integrating "learned research" with "applied research" in your field placements. However, during your advanced or second year, you will further your understanding and continue your discovery of the correlation between practice and scientific inquiry as you learn different methods by which to engage in research-informed practice and obtain the needed tools for practice-informed research.

Qualitative and quantitative research methods are two techniques and guidelines that can aid you in the utilization of evidence-based research. *Qualitative research* can be seen as a set of theoretical ideas and experiential methods for recognizing and describing various human experiences in which results are based on observations made in the field and analyzed in non-statistical ways that cannot be measured in the traditional sense. It also encompasses a descriptive analysis of data that involves process, meaning and understanding through spoken or written words such as in interviews, and/or observable behaviors (Bloom, Fischer, & Orme, 2009). As advanced or second year MSW students, you will learn different techniques for qualitative research design and various methods for conducting relevant qualitative analysis, including: participant observation, intensive interviewing, and focus groups (Marczyk, DeMatte, & Festinger, 2005). You will learn that qualitative research has many approaches, some of which include methods such as inductive reasoning, in which you build abstractions, concepts, hypotheses, and theories from details; and descriptive write-ups that involve fieldwork in which you conduct the research in sites that observe and record behavior in their natural environments (Marshall & Rossman, 2011).

Some of the methods or research designs of qualitative research include participant observations, key informant interviews, and focus groups. You will learn that participant observations include the gathering of data that involves developing a sustained relationship with individuals while they go about their normal activities. Key informant interviews are used to gather extremely detailed information from a small sample or a one-on-one basis with individuals. A focus group, also known as group interviewing, is used to gather preliminary information for a research study or to accumulate data concerning research questions. Conversely, *quantitative research* can be seen as the traditional form of research that involves the systematic empirical investigation of data from a representative sample of respondents in which statistical analysis is used to summarize and reduce data to understandable generalizations in identifying relationships (Rubin & Babbie, 2008). During your advanced or second year, you will engage in research-informed practice and practice-informed research as you learn to use the experiences you gain in your classroom to inform scientific inquiry and to use your evidence-based research learned from your agency field experiences to inform practice.

PRACTICE RESEARCH AND ASSESS OUTCOMES

This section will help further your understanding of the practice behaviors for the 2008 CSWE EPAS 2.1.6. *Engage in research-informed practice and practice-informed research*: (1) use practice experience to inform scientific inquiry, and (2) use research evidence to inform practice. The questions in this section are deliberately varied and randomly placed regarding the two research-based practice behaviors.

Multiple Choice

(Note: On the lines below each multiple choice question, explain why you chose that particular answer.)

Difficulty Scale: ✵ = Easy   ✵ ✵ = Moderate   ✵ ✵ ✵ = Challenging

1. Evan is a second year social work intern working at a large private advocacy agency that provides research to some of the major policy makers in your state. One of his clients asks about confidentiality at the agency, particularly when conducting research projects. The most appropriate step regarding his client's questions is for:

   a. Evan to explain that confidentiality is basically unimportant.
   b. Evan to remain silent to keep the confidentiality of the agency's procedures.
   c. Evan to explain the limitations of confidentiality.
   d. Evan to state that everything is completely confidential.

   Difficulty: ✵ = Easy
   Topic: Engage in practice-informed research
   Practice Behavior: Use practice experience to inform scientific inquiry

   _____

   _____

2. James is conducting a research study that asks about drinking behaviors at Historical Black Colleges and Universities (HBCUs). He is able to secure four seniors and three graduate students at one of the local HBCUs for his study. To support his hypothesis by answering ten open-ended questions, James gathers extremely detailed information from a small sample of two and some further information on a one-on-one basis with his research participants. James is:

   a. Researching the drinking behaviors at HBCUs utilizing the quantitative research method with a research design of participant observations.
   b. Conducting his research on the drinking behaviors at HBCUs utilizing the qualitative research method with a research design of focus groups.
   c. Researching the drinking behaviors on HBCUs utilizing the qualitative research method with a research design of participant observations.

d. Conducting his research on the drinking behaviors on HBCUs utilizing the quantitative research method with a research design of focus groups.

Difficulty: ✵ = Easy
Topic: Engage in research-informed practice
Practice Behavior: Use research evidence to inform practice

_____

_____

3. James, an advanced social work student, plans to study the attitude and behaviors in parenting styles of single welfare mothers living at an extended-stay hotel. The most effective method to collect data is:

   a. For James to contact social service case mangers.
   b. For James to ask a homeless shelter coordinator.
   c. For James to ask active residents of the extended-stay hotel about their attitudes and behaviors.
   d. For James to administer a questionnaire to every single mother at the local extended-stay hotel.

Difficulty: ✵ = Easy
Topic: Engage in research-informed practice
Practice Behavior: Use research evidence to inform practice

_____

_____

4. Nick is conducting a research project with an organization utilizing focus groups to gather data and the participants were asked to secure room(s) that maintain the confidentiality of the participants. The consent forms were read aloud and questions answered, for which written consent from parents or guardians was obtained for children under the age of eighteen and consent was obtained from the youth. Approximately nine participants are in the group. Nick is conducting a:

   a. Focus group with parents/guardians and children eighteen years of age and younger using quantitative research methods.
   b. Focus group with children eighteen years of age and younger utilizing qualitative research methods.
   c. Focus group with children's parents or guardians only utilizing quantitative research methods.

d. Focus group with children's parents or guardians and children eighteen years of age and younger utilizing qualitative research methods.

Difficulty: ✳ = Easy
Topic: Engage in practice-informed research
Practice Behavior: Use practice experience to inform scientific inquiry

_____

_____

5. Lafayette is a social work intern in her last semester at a social service agency in your community. She has a reputation for practicing the same treatment modality for every client regardless of its effectiveness because it is the most familiar to her and she likes it. She is currently working with a client who is showing little to no progress. From past experiences, Felicia, her supervisor, realizes the importance of utilizing other techniques that result in the most success for client interventions. Felicia has the responsibility to intervene if she sees that Lafayette always uses the same method, in particular if it is not helping the client. Felicia's first step regarding Lafayette's current practice behavior should be to:

   a. Have Lafayette research or Google other methods.
   b. Co-therapy the case with Lafayette and model a new method.
   c. Schedule Lafayette to attend a workshop to learn new methods.
   d. Take over the case from Lafayette to prevent any harm to the client.

Difficulty: ✳ ✳ = Moderate
Topic: Engage in research-informed practice
Practice Behavior: Use research evidence to inform practice

_____

_____

6. Jocelyn, a second year MSW student, is conducting field research in the home of children who are having problems with inattentiveness, overactivity, and impulsivity and are diagnosed with childhood attention deficit hyperactivity disorder (ADHD). She observes four-year-old Joe every hour for ten minutes for three days. After three days, she alternatively offers Joe chocolate chip cookies or a new toy truck, if Joe is able to sit still. The approach that Jocelyn has adopted, allowing for the gathering of data while developing a sustained relationship with Joe within the context of his normal activities, is best known as:

   a. Qualitative research.
   b. Quantitative program evaluation.
   c. Participant observation.

d. Quasi-experimental-design research.

Difficulty: ✕✕✕ = Challenging
Topic: Engage in research-informed practice
Practice Behavior: Use research evidence to inform practice

_____

_____

7. Parker is in his last semester of his advanced or second year and is interested in researching race relations before he graduates from the program. Which of the following is Parker's most appropriate and best possibility to engage in research-informed practices for field research?

    a. Research the effects of a course on racial relations on attitudes of students in a course at his university.

    b. Read about the differences in racial attitudes between students in two schools.

    c. Write a research paper on the change in racial relations as a result of an African American U.S. president.

    d. Follow a young white family through the years to trace changing patterns of race relations.

Difficulty: ✕✕✕ = Challenging
Topic: Engage in research-informed practice
Practice Behavior: Use research evidence to inform practice

_____

_____

8. You are known for your area of specialization regarding working with children of divorced or separated families. You are assigned a case in which the parents of a seven-year-old boy are temporarily separated because of the father's verbally abusive behavior toward the family, and the mother takes primary custody. The father's parents live in the same neighborhood, and he moves in with them, which allows for frequent overnight visits. The parents continue to argue and fight whenever they are together, which causes their son to act out at school. What is the best method that would allow you to employ evidence-based interventions as you evaluate your past practice behaviors in working with this family?

    a. Understand that no two cases are alike; create new strategies and methods in dealing with this family.

    b. Interview other family members in their neighborhood who are in situations of separation similar to that of your current clients.

    c. Speak with your supervisor, who is licensed and more experienced, for direction in developing a strategy for helping this family.

d. Review some of your similar cases and examine how you developed means by which the parents learned to constructively address conflicts and ways in which they focused on the needs of their children, and implement some of those strategies.

Difficulty: ✲✲✲ = Challenging
Topic: Engage in research-informed practice
Practice Behavior: Use research evidence to inform practice

_____

_____

9. Melanie, a second year social work student, is conducting research at her field placement agency. She is interested in criminology and the penal system with a concentration on parolees' perception of institutional rules and regulations. Melanie has only fifteen weeks to conduct her research. The study design that would be the most effective and practical is for Melanie to:

a. Conduct a qualitative research design with parolees that encompasses descriptive analysis of data obtained by way of methods such as spoken or written words, as in focus groups and/or key informant interviews.

b. Utilize and adopt quantitative research designs of descriptive write-ups that involve fieldwork that she conducts with parolees in their natural environments.

c. Utilize any combination of quantitative and qualitative research design over a period of five years.

d. Conduct a quantitative research design by utilizing inductive reasoning in which she builds abstractions, concepts, hypotheses, and theories from details.

Difficulty: ✲✲ = Moderate
Topic: Engage in research-informed practice
Practice Behavior: Use research evidence to inform practice

_____

_____

10. Quanah is in her second year of her MSW program and is interested in the prevention and care service needs of HIV-positive youth living in Georgia as well as that of their parents/guardians. The best form of inquiry in order to gather an in-depth understanding of this client base would be:

a. For Quanah to conduct field research with HIV-positive youth, and their parents or guardians, living in Georgia.

b. For Quanah to contact all of the private AIDS service organizations (ASOs) in the state of Georgia and ascertain their perception of the service utilization of HIV-positive adult males.

c. Due to the difficult nature of research, Quanah should contact her research professor for advice and recommendations concerning steps to take.

d. For Quanah to use any research method that assists her in generating knowledge from past similar research experiences that informs current practice.

Difficulty: ✲✲ ✲✲ = Moderate

Topic: Engage in practice-informed research

Practice Behavior: Use practice experience to inform scientific inquiry

_____

_____

Essay Questions

1. Identify and discuss three of the six steps to scientific inquiry and give an example of how you have experienced or seen each of them practiced.

2. Provide your understanding of the qualitative research method and identify two of three research designs and provide examples of each.

3. Discuss why and how using your experience to inform scientific inquiry helps your practice as an advanced or second year MSW student.

4. Discuss how the use of your experience to inform scientific inquiry and evidence-based research to inform practice better assists you in engaging in research-informed practice and practice-informed research.

Role-Play Exercise: "I Can Research That for You!"

Actions and responses to the role-play "I Can Research That for You!" will vary and depend on your individual characteristics, personal experience, and professional knowledge and are from your own perspective. Learn and enjoy!

You are a social worker director of an AIDS service organization (ASO) and speculate about the changing needs of HIV-positive youth ages thirteen to twenty-four. The director of the ASO questions the effectiveness of some of your therapy regarding (1) several clients' alleged inappropriate use of several social network media and your response to their behavior; (2) the maturity level of the clients thirteen to eighteen years of age as compared to nineteen to twenty-four years regarding attitude and behavior toward HIV-positive status; and (3) the clients' service-utilization patterns.

In seeking answers to these questions, role-play the process of developing an inquiry in attempting to engage in research-informed practice and practice-informed research. All participants must role-play how they would go about using evidence-based research to inform practice and experience to inform scientific inquiry.

Practice with MySocialWorkLab

Visit **MySocialWorkLab** at www.mysocialworklab.com to watch these competency-based videos.

Watch

Research-Based Practice—**Engaging in Research Informed Practice**

Research-Based Practice—**Contracting with the Client to Select an Evidence-Based Therapy**

References

Bloom, M., Fischer, J., & Orme, J. (2009). *Evaluating practice: Guidelines for the accountable professional* (6th Ed.). Boston: Allyn & Bacon.

Marczyk, G., DeMatte, D., & Festinger, D. (2005). *Essentials of research design and methodology.* Hoboken: Wiley.

Marshall, C., & Rossman, G. B. (2011). *Designing qualitative research* (5th Ed.). London: Sage.

Rubin, A., & Babbie, E. (2008). *Research methods for social work* (6th Ed.). Belmont: Brooks/Cole.

CSWE EPAS **2.1.7** *Apply knowledge of human behavior and the social environment*

Human behavior is the seventh core competency of the 2008 EPAS and provides a solid foundation to build upon as an advanced or second year social work student. In your advanced or second year, you will become knowledgeable about the behavior of your clients across the life cycle and the range of social systems in which they live. As a core competency, human behavior seeks to find ways in which social systems promote or deter maintaining or achieving the health and well-being of your clients. You will begin to understand how to apply theories and knowledge from the liberal arts as a means to understanding biological, social, psychological, and spiritual development.

You will also learn that human behavior and the social environment are important to understand for successful and effective social work practice. You will learn methods for understanding how clients interact both with one another and within their environment, as well as how they are affected by these interactions. You will learn about the interrelationships between individual behavior and larger social environments, including your review of a number of theories and concepts that explain human behavior and social undercurrents that affect the lives of your client base.

You will utilize conceptual frameworks and a series of steps that guide the processes of assessment and intervention, as well as evaluation regarding the application of knowledge of the human behavior and social environment of your client base.

USING CONCEPTUAL FRAMEWORKS TO GUIDE ASSESSMENT, INTERVENTION, AND EVALUATION

The clients that social workers serve are often burdened with fearsome and demoralizing problems and social ills, such as homelessness, disease, mental disablement, and discrimination.

During your advanced or second year, you will learn how to utilize conceptual frameworks that will guide your assessment, intervention, and evaluation of the human behavior within the social environment of your client base. One of the many models you will learn that will guide your thinking about human behavior within the social environment is the *systems theory approach*. The systems theory approach provides a method by which to understand various systems and how clients interact with them. Systems may include the individual within the context of a family, the family within a context of small groups, or an individual within the context of an organization and the community or social institution, such as an agency or church.

You will also learn to distinguish between various levels of interventions, such as client-level interventions and system-level interventions. *Client-level interventions* involve direct communication with clients as you coordinate services on their behalf and include the development of services. *System-level interventions*, on the other hand, involve the behind-the-scenes work that evaluates already existing interventions and strategies that work toward improving, for example, your clients' human behavior within the context of their social environment.

You will better understand and apply conceptual frameworks that guide your evaluation as you come to understand the correlation between evaluations and research when conceptualizing frameworks that guide you in your practice. Although both collect and analyze data, evaluation is known to relate to practice, whereas research relates more to academics. Gredler (1996) espouses that the differences between evaluation and research lie within a number of distinguishing characteristics and explains that educational research's purpose is to test principles and theories that may be generalizable across space and time; and researchers determine the nature of the programs to be investigated. Patton (1997) suggests that evaluation differs from research in the purpose of data collection and standards for judging quality and that evaluation is always deductive because it is based on actions people took intentionally to produce expected results.

CRITIQUING AND APPLYING KNOWLEDGE TO UNDERSTAND PEOPLE AND THEIR ENVIRONMENT

Critiquing, evaluating, or assessing knowledge to understand people and their environment are highly variable and depend on the professional observer. During your advanced or second year as MSW student practitioners, you will further your understanding of the importance of the increased responsibility to document and record the effectiveness of interventions utilized in the service of your clients at your field agency practicum. You will learn that a broad range of skills is needed when working with clients and that knowing methods of critiquing, evaluating, and assessing strengths and limitations provide the utmost value to understanding clients within the context of their environment. As frontline student practitioners and future staff members of agencies and organizations, you will further your understanding of basic concepts and various dimensions to critiquing knowledge.

During your advanced or second year, you will learn to (1) recognize that which you do not understanding regarding the human behavior of your clients; and (2) identify the cause or causes of your lack of understanding, which will allow you to create a set of criteria by which to make value-critical judgments regarding your quest for knowledge to understand your client and their environment in the delivery of service to them. Social work is unique for its simultaneous focus on the client and social environment, and your understanding of the service delivery system will provide you the opportunity to critique and/or assess your knowledge to understand your clients and their environment. By advancing your understanding of the service delivery systems, you will become more accountable regarding the application of your knowledge, which will in turn improve your response time and the manner in which you apply knowledge of human behavior and the social environment.

During your advanced or second year, you will further your understanding of your clients within their environment and advance your foundational comprehension of knowledge base. *Knowledge base* can be understood as the knowledge domain or the content of a particular field of study; however, you will come to understand that knowledge base in social work education can also refer to the body of principles, concepts, and procedures that are widely recognized and used when trying to understand the various human behaviors of clients. There are many components and levels to applying knowledge to understand clients and their environment, some of which include empirically-based knowledge and practice-based knowledge (Rogers, 2006). As advanced or second year MSW students, you will learn that *empirically-based knowledge* is the knowledge generated from various types of formal, systematic research, whether involving experiments, large-scale surveys, or case studies. It is often based on direct observation in which the techniques and methods used are clearly outlined, so much so that they are replicable by other researchers in future similar studies. It is also often used to provide the most informed, effective, and reliable information on issues to help guide practice (Rogers, 2006; Schriver, 2011).

Practice-based knowledge, also known as "practice wisdom" is a specific level of understanding engendered from practice experience. You will learn that practice-based knowledge is often not codified into practice theories and tested empirically but is typically regarded as the body of practice principles or "tricks of the trade" that are a fundamental part of the social work culture (Rogers, 2006).

By understanding the concept of knowledge and the different components and/or levels that it offers, such as empirically-based and practice-based knowledge, you will began to understand ways of applying knowledge as a method to understanding clients and their environments.

PRACTICE APPLYING HUMAN BEHAVIOR AND ASSESSING OUTCOMES

This section will help further your understanding of the 2008 CSWE EPAS 2.1.7. *Apply knowledge of human behavior and the social environment.* It will help you to apply knowledge of human behavior and the social environment in your practice as you (1) utilize conceptual frameworks to guide the processes of assessment, intervention, and evaluation; and (2) critique and apply knowledge to understand person and environment. The questions in this section are deliberately varied and randomly placed regarding the two human behavior practice behaviors.

Multiple Choice

(Note: On the lines below each multiple-choice question, explain why you chose that particular answer.)

Difficulty Scale: ✲ = Easy   ✲ ✲ = Moderate   ✲ ✲ ✲ = Challenging

1. Gloria is a recent graduate from an MSW program from the state school in your city and is has secured employment at a local social service agency. One of her first tasks in her new position is to develop the skill level of several of her new colleagues who recently graduated with their BSWs, based on a set of pre-established competencies. To assist in this process, Gloria's best option is to:

    a. Suggest to the director that contracting with an expert to individually speak with the recent graduates would be the best move to make.
    b. Call a staff meeting to pool ideas for the recent graduates.
    c. Design a training program based on the required competencies.
    d. Recommend attendance at a workshop offered by the state.

    Difficulty: ✲ ✲ = Moderate
    Topic: Using conceptual frameworks to guide assessment, intervention, and evaluation
    Practice Behavior: Using conceptual frameworks to guide intervention

    _____

    _____

2. Steven is a second year MSW student interning at OK Counseling, a local social services agency that specializes in working with youth who have suffered the death of a parent. He is counseling Cathy, an eight-year-old who is struggling with the sudden death of her father as a result of a plane accident and is concerned that she failed to give him a good-luck kiss before he traveled. Steven has had several cases such as Cathy's and is tapping into his practice-based knowledge as he applies practice wisdom in understanding Cathy's behavior and response to her father's accident. Cathy is more likely to:

    a. Feel hostile toward her mother.
    b. To attribute the death of her father to something mysterious and dangerous.

   c. To feel anger toward authority figures.

   d. Attribute the death of her father to something she had done or failed to do.

Difficulty: ❄ = Easy
Topic: Applying knowledge to understand people and their environment
Practice Behavior: Critiquing and applying knowledge to understand people and their environment

_____

_____

3. Flora is a recent MSW graduate working as an employee-assistance program counselor for one of the largest retail stores in the world. She has heard rumors that Jim, an employee, has been complaining about being uncomfortable in his work environment because of the possible inappropriate behavior of a sexual nature by one of the top officials in the company. Flora should:

   a. Refer Jim to the company's legal department.

   b. Disregard the rumor and explore Jim's concerns only when he approaches her about them.

   c. Confront the top official about the rumor in hopes of protecting the company's image.

   d. Explore whether Jim's feelings are affecting his job performance.

Difficulty: ❄ ❄ = Moderate
Topic: Critiquing knowledge to understand people and their environment
Practice Behavior: Critiquing and applying knowledge to understand people and their environment

_____

_____

4. Miller is a social work intern at the Regional Youth Detention Center and is trying to assess the behavior and response of Julian, a twelve-year-old middle-class male, in his initial reaction to the detention center. Julian will more than likely respond by:

   a. Clinging to Miller.

   b. Experiencing anxiety.

c. Running away.

d. Throwing a tantrum.

Difficulty: ✲ = Easy

Topic: Critiquing knowledge to understand people and their environment

Practice Behavior: Critiquing and applying knowledge to understand people and their environment

_____

_____

5. Lucy's parents died when she was two-years-old and she was placed in several different foster homes from ages three to fourteen. She suffered a date rape at age seventeen that resulted in her first pregnancy. She got married to Desi at age twenty-two and later had four additional children. At age thirty-two, she learns of her husband's infidelity and begins to neglect her family by spending an inordinate amount of time on Facebook and going out socially with her female friends. Lucy's main issue that contributes to her behavior has to do with:

a. Trusting people due to past rejections.

b. Intimacy with her husband, Desi.

c. Identifying with herself.

d. The lack of affection for her children.

Difficulty: ✲ = Easy

Topic: Using conceptual frameworks to guide assessment

Practice Behavior: Using conceptual frameworks to guide assessment, intervention, and evaluation

_____

_____

6. You work at the local Community Service Board (CSB) and are providing therapy to Pattie. Pattie has agreed to participate in a new research study in which therapy will be conducted remotely and recorded via the Internet. She has also been provided with a computer that has video capability and Internet services, all funded by the research. As a result of her participation in the research project, Pattie also pays only 15 percent of the counseling fee, while the research project will pay the remaining 85 percent. Pattie signed a twelve-month commitment agreement indicating that she understood the research program and its requirements. Eleven months into the project, Pattie tells you that she does not want to participate in the research project; however, she would like to continue treatment. Your best response is to:

a. Share with Pattie that continuation in treatment is linked to continued participation.

b. Share with Pattie that she can make a choice to end participation at any time, and help her by referring her for continued treatment with another therapist.

c. Say nothing in the hope that Pattie will realize she has less than a month left in the project.

d. Point out to Pattie that she received certain benefits and she is morally obliged to fulfill the terms of the agreement.

Difficulty: ✸✸✸ = Challenging
Topic: Using conceptual frameworks to guide evaluation
Practice Behavior: Using conceptual frameworks to guide assessment, intervention, and evaluation

_____

_____

7. You are the discussion leader for a group of residents of a poverty area, many of whom are against a proposal to locate a group home for drug-addicted boys in their neighborhood. The best way for you to assist the group is to help them first:

a. Get to know one another on an informal basis highlighting their thoughts about protecting young men from a life of drugs.

b. Understand the overall background of the drug problem and the need for such a facility in the community.

c. Discuss the pros and cons briefly, take a vote, and accept the decision of the majority.

d. Get to know one another on an informal basis, highlighting their views on the need for a second chance for the boys.

Difficulty: ✸✸ = Moderate
Topic: Applying knowledge to understand people and their environment
Practice Behavior: Critiquing and applying knowledge to understand people and their environment

_____

_____

8. Jonathan is a second year MSW intern at the Department of Family and Children Services in your county. In his efforts to use evaluation with regard to his clients' human behavior within the context of their social environment, he has learned that a major criticism of casework is that it:

a. Does not produce social-change legislation.

b. Is less effective than group work, as proven by the success of self-helpers.

c. Follows the medical model.

d. Addresses the individual and therefore doesn't produce change in the environment.

Difficulty: ✲ = Easy
Topic: Using conceptual frameworks to guide evaluation
Practice Behavior: Using conceptual frameworks to guide assessment, intervention, and evaluation

_____

_____

9. Mitchell is a thirteen-year-old male whose parents divorced when he was five years old. However, the parents remained friends and co-parented Mitchell. He is perceived to be loved by both his mother and father, and he loves them. You are counseling him because he shares that he feels that he is dominated by them. As he gets older, he is likely to:

a. Turn to drugs.
b. Rebel against authority.
c. Drop out of school.
d. Regress to a time when he was more independent.

Difficulty: ✲ = Easy
Topic: Applying knowledge to understand people and their environment
Practice Behavior: Critiquing and applying knowledge to understand people and their environment

_____

_____

10. Franklin, an LMSW, has recently gained employment with a social service agency that specializes in divorce arbitration. Assigned to his caseload are Jonas and Elizabeth Kay, a couple considering divorce due to their very combative and disagreement-prone relationship. They are considered to be well-to-do and pride themselves on their ability to provide for the current and future financial needs of their two children, Carl, age fourteen, and Cooper, age twelve. In Franklin's attempts to use conceptual frameworks to guide his line of intervention for the Kay family, he should first try to:

a. Make viable plans for Carl and Cooper.
b. Mediate until Jonas and Elizabeth are better able to deal with each other.

    c. Help Jonas and Elizabeth divide their property equally.

    d. Assess strengths and weaknesses in the couple's negotiations.

Difficulty: ✳ ✳ ✳ = Challenging

Topic: Using conceptual frameworks to guide intervention

Practice Behavior: Using conceptual frameworks to guide assessment, intervention, and evaluation

---

Essay Questions

1. Discuss how your use of conceptual framework helps guide assessment and intervention in your efforts to apply knowledge of human behavior and the social environment.

2. Discuss how the utilization of conceptual or theoretical constructs aid in guiding the evaluation of your clients within the context of their social environment, and identify two possible levels of intervention that might assist you in your conceptual framework.

3. Discuss several ways in which you can critique knowledge to understand your clients and their environment in your field placements during your advanced or second year within your MSW program.

4. Identify and discuss at least two ways in which you can apply knowledge to understand your client within the context of his or her environment.

Role-Play Exercise: "Human Behavior—To Be or Not To Be!"

Actions and responses to the role-play "Human Behavior—To Be or Not To Be" will vary and depend on your individual characteristics, personal experience, and professional knowledge and are from your own perspective. Learn and enjoy!

    You are interning at a social service agency that provides 24 hour crisis intervention services to call-in and walk-in clients within your community. You usually work from 9:00 a.m. to 5:00 p.m. but are requested to make up some hours and were available only during the second shift, 5:00 p.m. to 11:00 p.m., when you will be without the direct assistance of your agency supervisor. During your shift, an African American client in crisis walks into your agency and tells you that she and her twelve-year-old daughter discontinued taking medication for their HIV/AIDS status because they have been healed supernaturally. However, she believes that her daughter is lacking in faith for her healing because she has been unable to keep food in her system for two weeks and is losing weight rapidly.

In exploring this scenario, role-play the process of responding to the mother's crisis and consider (1) what conceptual framework you will utilize to guide your assessment; and (2) the interventions and techniques you will use when applying you knowledge of human behavior to understand your client and their environment.

Practice with MySocialWorkLab

Visit **MySocialWorkLab** at www.mysocialworklab.com to watch these competency-based videos.

Watch

Human Behavior—**The Ecological Model Using the Friere Method**

Human Behavior—**Developing an Action Plan that Changes the Internal and External**

References

Gredler, M. E. (1996). *Program evaluation.* Englewood Cliffs, NJ: Prentice Hall.

Patton, M. W. (1997). *Utilization-focused evaluation: The new century test.* Thousand Oaks, CA: Sage.

Rogers, A. T. (2006). *Human behavior in the social environment.* New York: McGraw-Hill.

Schriver, J. M. (2011). *Human behavior and the social environment: Shifting paradigms in essential knowledge for social work practice* (5th Ed.). Boston: Pearson Education/Allyn & Bacon.

8

POLICY PRACTICE

CSWE EPAS **2.1.8** *Engage in policy practice to advance social and economic well-being and to deliver effective social work services*

Policy practice is the eighth core competency of the 2008 EPAS and provides a solid foundation to build upon as an advanced or second year social work student. You learned during your foundation year that policy drives practice and is the engine behind the successful development and delivery of services. However, during your advanced or second year, you will learn strategies that enable you to actively engage in policy practice while at your agency placement sites. You will also further your knowledge of policy practice by increasing your understanding of the history of social work and its current structures of social policies and services. You will begin to better comprehend the role of policy in service delivery, as well as the role of practice in policy development.

During your foundation year, you mastered an understanding of the terms and key concepts of social policy. However, in your advanced or second year, you will realize that the correlation between practice and policy development is an important concept to understand. You will further your understanding of how to engage in policy practices that advance social and economic well-being. You will also begin to analyze policy that advances social well-being, as well as formulate policies that attempt to improve the social well-being of your clients. In your advanced or second year MSW programs, you will demonstrate the ability to use advocacy skills at all levels of practice to enhance service delivery to children, youth, and families and to engage in policy development as a change agent.

As you begin to adopt steps that assist in advocating policies that advanced social well-being you will collaborate with both colleagues and clients for effective policy actions as you demonstrate the capacity to analyze, formulate, and advocate for realistic alternative policies for your clients when implicated.

ANALYZING, FORMULATING, AND ADVOCATING FOR POLICIES

In analyzing policies in social work, you will begin to understand the historical role of social work in the development of policies; and acquire a degree of knowledge regarding specific federal, state, and local public policies, laws, and court decisions that affect practice and service delivery to your clients. In your advanced or second year programs, you will further your understanding of the socioeconomic, ideological, and political issues impacting social work and the various types of polices involved in the practice of the professions and the impact that certain legislation, such as the Multiethnic Placement Act (MEPA), plays in analyzing policy.

The Multiethnic Placement Act of 1994 (MEPA) was designed to prohibit discrimination in adoption and foster care when trying to locate placement for a child, based on ethnicity. MEPA provided a remedy under the Civil Rights Act of 1964 for potential foster or adoptive parents who believe they may have been discriminated against by adoption workers and required the Department of Health and Human Services (DHHS) to provide guidance to agencies and entities so that they can be in compliance with MEPA (Curtis & Alexander, 2010; Farley, 2010). MEPA was later amended by the Interethnic Adoptions Provisions Act (IEP). The IEP Act made MEPA apply to all child welfare agencies, private adoption agencies, and foster care agencies. Prior to MEPA, children were not allowed to be fostered or adopted transracially. This was a huge disservice to the children in care awaiting adoption.

In your second or advanced year, you will begin to understand that there are different means by which policies are formulated in social work. You will learn that policies essentially are proposed courses or regulations imposed by policy planning agencies and government organizations at the local, federal, or national levels that inform practice behaviors. You will formulate an understanding of agency policies through the lens of different practice behaviors that result from various federal laws and amendments, such as the Adoption and Safe Families Act of 1997 (ASFA). In formulating agency policy, it is important to know the purpose and the intent of the law or act that drives the practice of the agency policy.

For example, the purpose of the federal Adoption and Safe Families Act of 1997 (ASFA) is to expedite permanency planning and set time limits for a child's stay in foster care. ASFA sets a time limit on the "reasonable efforts" that are taken by a social service agency to rehabilitate a family so that the child can return to the biological family/parents.

When a child has been in foster care or in a placement for fifteen to twenty-two months, the state has to terminate the parental rights of the child unless the child is placed with relatives. Parental rights will not be terminated if there is a "compelling reason not to file such an action or when services have not been provided to the family" (Chambers & Wedel, 2009; Shireman, 2003).

The intended twofold effect of ASFA is to (1) revitalize the child welfare system so that agencies can provide services to a child or children as soon as possible after becoming involved with the them; and (2) galvanize the parent(s) so that they become involved with the child welfare system in order to work their case plan and become involved in making life better for the child.

During your advanced or second year, you will learn that advocating for policies entails many steps, one of which is focusing upon analyzing selected federal, state, and local policies specifically relevant to the continuum of your particular area of interest and specification regarding practice and service delivery. Your advanced year will provide a framework for the analysis of family policies in terms of a social justice perspective that emphasizes equality of opportunity and access to education, housing, jobs, and services; the values that underlie contemporary family policies; exclusionary consequences; and their implications for promotion or undermining of family cohesion.

Moreover, you will learn to analyze the organizational structure of social policy within welfare agencies while focusing on the leadership roles of social workers, managers, and administrators to influence policy advocacy and implementation. You will learn that the advocating of policies such as AFSA and MEPA will force the practice of social work in terms of expediting services to clients such as parents and will motivate them to finish their court-ordered case plan in a timely manner. It also forces the various departments involved to make reasonable efforts in placing children in a timely manner and in providing service to the family. You will learn that advocating for policies entails your interacting and delivery of services at all levels of practice, such as in the micro, mezzo, and macro, depending on the needs of your client base.

COLLABORATING WITH OTHERS FOR EFFECTIVE POLICY ACTION

You will learn during your advanced or second year that many federal, state and local policy issues confronting social workers require collaboration with other disciplines and professions. You will learn about legislation regulations and the importance of interfacing with and developing working collaborative relationships between legislatures, communities, and organizations in order to create effective policy action. You will learn of the role of social class, and ethnic, racial, and cultural diversity, in the formulation of policy and in the application of policy. An agency should also note the willingness of the local community and other outside organizations to help out. The agency should look at their own capabilities (e.g., having a culturally competent staff) (Chambers & Wedel, 2009).

An agency should be aware of the relationship they already have with the community; having an idea if they are liked or not can indicate whether or not the collaboration will be successful. The agency should note whether or not the community or population knows that the agency exists and the agency goals.

The agency should raise public awareness by promoting their practice and the agency's goal or mission, because if the community is not aware, collaboration will not be successful. The agency should also look at the community's willingness to work with them in an effort to collaborate with others for effective policy action.

PRACTICE POLICY ENGAGEMENT AND ASSESS OUTCOMES

This section will help further your understanding of the practice behaviors for the 2008 CSWE EPAS 2.1.8. *Engage in policy practice to advance social and economic well-being and to deliver effective social work services*: (1) analyze, formulate, and advocate for policies that advance social well-being; and (2) collaborate with colleagues and clients for effective policy action. The questions in this section are deliberately varied and randomly placed regarding the two research-based practice behaviors.

Multiple Choice

(Note: On the lines below each multiple-choice question, explain why you chose that particular answer.)

Difficulty Scale: ✳ = Easy   ✳ ✳ = Moderate   ✳ ✳ ✳ = Challenging

1. Jackie, a second year social work student, is working with a group of residents at the OK Nursing Home, where her seventy-nine-year-old grandmother Sarah Lee lives. Sarah Lee and several of her friends want their voices heard about the treatment that they have been receiving at one of the local coffee shops and feel that the best place to express their concerns would be at one of the upcoming state legislative sessions. As a second year social work student, Jackie should first:

   a. Assess the residents' strengths and weaknesses.
   b. Help residents develop advocacy skills.
   c. Discuss consequences of failure to achieve their goal.
   d. Recommend material on conflict resolution.

   Difficulty: ✳ = Easy
   Topic: Advocate
   Practice behavior: Advocate for policies that advance social well-being

   _____

   _____

2. Joshua is an LCSW at Spiritual Assemblies Group Home, a private foster home funded and run by a two Christian local churches. Intern Joan comes into Joshua's office with thirteen-year-old Paul, who disregards weekend curfew and fails to attend weekly Bible study, both of which are important policies of the group home. The policies at Spiritual Assemblies are very clear and strict regarding residents who fail to follow the rules. The best thing for intern Joan to do regarding this situation is:

   a. Request that Joshua explain the policies as well as the religious beliefs of the Christian faith and provide her with knowledge so she can understand the situation and better work with Paul.
   b. Go to one of the religious Elders for advice in the situation.
   c. Send Paul to a child psychologist for testing and consultation regarding his oppositional defiant behavior.

d. Review the policies of Spiritual Assemblies Group Home and read a book about the Christian faith and its beliefs regarding following rules.

Difficulty: ✿ ✿ = Moderate
Topic: Policy collaboration
Practice Behavior: Collaborate with colleagues and clients for effective policy action

_____

_____

3. Alex is interning at the County Juvenile Court and provides anger-management services to first-time offenders. Marcus has been mandated to receive ten hours of anger management, which Alex will provide, due to his alleged outbursts and behaviors at school. They have had two sessions, but Marcus has said nothing when asked questions. The next best step for Alex to take is to:

   a. Refer Marcus to another counselor within the court system.
   b. Decide whether or not Marcus is willing to undergo treatment.
   c. Acknowledge to Marcus that there is some reluctance and advocate for another form of treatment, such as group therapy.
   d. Confront Alex concerning the reason for his referral.

Difficulty: ✿ ✿ = Moderate
Topic: Analyze and advocate
Practice Behavior: Analyze, formulate, and advocate for policies that advance social well-being

_____

_____

4. Eighty-five-year-old Jessie, an elderly woman in your apartment complex, lives alone. She is of sound mind and was very active in the community and physically before she broke her hip. You and her landlord, James, are cohorts in the second year of your MSW program. James has recently reviewed the agreement of the lease and has threatened to evict Jessie because she has violated the rules of the lease, as her apartment is unkempt, dirty, and infested with pests. As Jessie's advocate, you would:

   a. Clean the apartment.
   b. Try to persuade the landlord to allow her to stay.
   c. Arrange home services to help Jessie manage her apartment.

d. Arrange for placement or a new apartment.

Difficulty: ✳ = Easy
Topic: Collaborate with client
Practice behavior: Collaborate with colleagues and clients for effective policy action

_____

_____

5. The most appropriate method by which to inform your supervisor of the effects of agency policies at your practicum site is by:

   a. Letting the supervisor know all of its faults.
   b. Discussing policies with other staff and feeding back complaints.
   c. Writing a memo to the director.
   d. Letting the supervisor know how it affects clients.

Difficulty: ✳ ✳ = Moderate
Topic: Collaborate for effective policy action
Practice Behavior: Collaborate with colleagues and clients for effective policy action

_____

_____

6. Kelvin owns Can Do for You, a social service agency that provides assistance with client environmental problems such as locating shelter, securing access to child care, helping clients with WIC (Women, Infants, and Children) applications, and securing legal representation or other supportive services for families. You are attempting to operationalize or explain to a potential client the category of services that Can Do offers. The best term to describe these services to the potential client is:

   a. Parallel services.
   b. Task-oriented services.
   c. Advocacy services.
   d. Indeterminate services.

Difficulty: ✳ = Easy
Topic Analyze and formulate
Practice Behavior: Analyze, formulate, and advocate for policies that advance social well-being

_____

_____

7. After speaking on child trafficking before a congregation at one of the mega-churches in your community, Josiah, a recent MSW, learned that the anchor from the community's largest news station grossly mistook and overstated his qualifications. As a result of the news coverage, a false impression was created, and Josiah has received many emails, texts, and calls from agencies soliciting him for consultation. In this case, the best action for Josiah should be to:

   a. Do nothing; he did not embellish his qualifications and can just benefit from the endorsement.
   b. Contact his state NASW ethics board and ask for guidance.
   c. Ask the news station to make a correction and inform the callers of the error.
   d. Call colleagues and let them know he was not responsible for the error.

   Difficulty: ✿ ✿ ✿ = Challenging
   Topic: Advocate for polices
   Practice Behavior: Analyze, formulate, and advocate for policies that advance social well-being

   _____

   _____

8. Lorenzo is a social worker for a local agency that assists clients in reapplying for Supplemental Security Income (SSI) after being denied by the Social Security Administration (SSA). He is concerned about a policy that his client Graham has educated him on regarding his eligibility that, when addressed, can alter Graham's life and those of Graham's children. To empower Graham, Lorenzo must:

   a. Solve the problem for Graham.
   b. Link Graham with resources that he needs to improve his life.
   c. Facilitate Graham's ability to independently solve problems.
   d. Agree with Graham's request for a specific service.

   Difficulty: ✿ ✿ ✿ = Challenging
   Topic: Advocate
   Practice Behavior: Analyze, formulate, and advocate for policies that advance social well-being

   _____

   _____

9. The assistant director has irrefutable evidence that the director of a large community fundraising agency has signed costly non-competitive contracts with a business in which the director has ownership interest.

These actions are against the policy of the agency and the standards of the board. The activity is unknown to the board of directors, violates agency policy, and may be illegal. The assistant director's first step is to:

a. Discuss the matter with other senior staff of the agency.
b. Discuss the matter with the director and then notify the district attorney.
c. Consult the agency's outside attorney.
d. Discuss the matter with the director and then notify the chairman of the board.

Difficulty: ✢✢ = Moderate
Topic: Collaborate with colleagues
Practice Behavior: Collaborate with colleagues and clients for effective policy action

_____

_____

10. After receiving vocational training through the Temporary Assistance to Needy Families program (TANF), Lisa succeeds in finding an entry-level job. Zack is a social worker at Restore Job Training, a social agency that specializes in providing vocational training to clients who apply for TANF. As a stipulation of eligibility for TANF benefits, clients applying for help are mandated to go to Restore Job Training. Within a short period of time, Lisa is promoted to a supervisory position and is feeling better about her life. Although her financial outlook has improved, her family situation remains problematic. Her nineteen-year-old son Frank is still staying at home, unemployed, and in and out of drug-treatment centers. Lisa is terrified that because of the new policy regarding drug offense, she might lose her home and return to her former life of being homeless and on public assistance. She realizes that if she does not continue to do well and become firm with her son Frank about his drug use, she might lose it all. As Lisa contemplates her situation, she grows increasingly anxious about holding on to her apartment and her current lifestyle. Zack, the social worker, should:

a. Work with Lisa to help her understand that her relationship with her son Frank is very taxing to her emotionally and financially and she should ask him to move out.
b. Suggest to Lisa that she discuss her situation with her employer. The worker should also help Lisa identify any legal employment protections available to her.
c. Help Lisa understand the role her son plays in sustaining her poor self-image.

d. Support Lisa and empathize with her situation, without offering any alternatives for her to consider.

Difficulty: ✭ ✭ ✭ = Challenging
Topic: Collaborate for effective policy action
Practice Behavior: Collaborate with colleagues and clients for effective policy action

_____

_____

Essay Questions

1. Discuss the role of policy in service delivery in relationship to the role of practice in policy development at your current internship agency.

2. Explain the Multiethnic Placement Act of 1994 (MEPA) and discuss how your understanding of it can better help you analyze policy development.

3. What does the acronym ASFA mean and how has it changed policy practice at the agency level?

4. How does collaborating with others affect policy actions? In your answer, provide an example of how you have demonstrated this in your field agency.

Role-Play Exercise: When Policy Interpretation and Service Delivery Clash!

Actions and responses to the role-play "When Policy Interpretation and Service Delivery Clash!" will vary and depend on your individual characteristics, personal experience, professional and knowledge and are from your own perspective. Learn and enjoy!

You are in the first week of you second semester of your advanced or second year MSW program and finally quit your job to concentrate on academics. Your spouse has been out of the home for two weeks on a business trip out of the country, and most of the money that the two of you budgeted for this month was earmarked for the international trip; hence, your funds are very limited. You have applied for food stamps with a new eligibility worker and have been deemed ineligible because of your spouse's income. You overhear several other people in the waiting room of the agency complaining that they just knew that they were eligible. You are very familiar with the means test requirements and know that you are eligible, and that the individuals complaining might be eligible, and you feel that because of the worker's lack of knowledge of the policies, many applications were wrongly denied.

Each participant must role-play how they would go about responding to this dilemma in terms of analyzing and advocating for policy development that utilizes the techniques and skills of critical thinking and results in the "best decision" for all parties.

This role-play exercise can take place in either a professional formal setting, such as in the waiting area of the agency, or a relaxed, casual setting, such as in a coffee shop. The minimum number of participants is three: (1) the student seeking help with food assistance; (2) the person who appears to be facilitating the conversation regarding the treatment from the worker; and (3) the other person listening.

Practice with MySocialWorkLab

Visit **MySocialWorkLab** at www.mysocialworklab.com to watch these competency-based videos.

Watch

Policy Practice—**Building Alliances**

Policy Practice—**Advocating for the Client**

Policy Practice—**Participating in Policy Changes**

References

Chambers, D. E., & Wedel, K. (2009). *Social policy and social programs: A method for the practical public policy analyst* (5th Ed.). Boston, MA: Allyn & Bacon.

Curtis, C. M., & Alexander, R., Jr. (2010). Correlates of African American children in and out of their families. *Families in Society, 91*(1), 85–90.

Farley, J. E. (2010). *Majority–minority relations* (6th Ed.). Upper Saddle River, NJ: Prentice-Hall.

Leiber, M. J. (2002). Disproportionate minority confinement (DMC) of youth: An analysis of state and federal efforts to address the issue. *Crime and Delinquency, 48*(1), 3–45.

Shireman, J. F. (2003). *Critical issues in child welfare.* New York: Columbia University Press.

9

PRACTICE CONTEXTS

CSWE EPAS **2.1.9** *Respond to contexts that shape practice*

Practice contexts is the ninth core competency EPAS and involves necessary knowledge, values, and skills that present a solid foundation to build upon as an advanced or second year social work student. You will learn that advanced knowledge of the various practice contexts during your second year is essential in shaping an informed and resourceful practice in the field at your individual practicums and critical to your ability to be proactive in responding to the evolving organizational environments at various level of practice. During your second or advanced year, you will learn the steps to becoming knowledgeable, creative, and practical in response to ever-changing community and societal contexts at all levels of practice. You will also learn how to become aware of the various practice dynamics and make use of your learned knowledge and skills to respond proactively to the needs of your client base.

In your foundation year, you learned the importance of your human behavior, policy, and research courses to practice. However, as advanced or second year MSW students, you will constantly realize, evaluate, and concentrate on the changing environments in which you will work; the populations you will serve; and the systematic and scientific developments relevant to your ability to provide services to your client base (EPAS, 2008). You will also be educated to understand emerging societal trends in providing relevant services, as well as strategies and techniques for providing leadership that promotes sustainable changes in service delivery to your perspective clients. You will learn that mastery of the practice context core competency will enable you to improve the quality of social services to your clients in the field at your perspective practicum agencies. As advanced or second year MSW students, you will further your understanding of the methods that will help you to respond to contexts that shape practice.

DISCOVERING, APPRAISING, AND ATTENDING TO CHANGES AND TRENDS TO PROVIDE RELEVANT SERVICES

During your foundation year, you learned steps to discovering changes and trends in providing relevant services to your clients. Protective services for abused and neglected children, services to schools, and services within mental health agencies have all been traditional places in which social workers delivered services. However, with the changing nature of human problems in the globalized world, you will begin to realize the relevance of services in practice context to immigrants and different religious/spiritual sects. During your advanced or second year, you will learn that social workers are oftentimes front-line service providers to immigrants, for whom they provide an array of services that are essential to assessing their individual needs.

You will come to understand that many of the services provided to immigrants address issues and experiences of trauma related to alienation, loneliness, language acquisition, discrimination, and economic displacement. As an advanced or second year MSW student practitioner, you will continue to learn the impact of spirituality and religion on your professional practice and methods by which to respond to contexts that shape practice. Religion and traditional spiritual practices have had considerable influences in the establishment of human service delivery in general and social work practice in particular within the United States (Morales, Sheafor & Scott, 2012). You will further learn that relevant services provided to clients who hold high religious and spiritual values tend to also include problems of social, political, and economic justice that are oftentimes intertwined with their individual spiritual and religious doctrines.

As first or foundation year MSW students, you learned steps to understanding the different environments in which your clients receive services. However, during your advanced or second year, you will learn how to appraise the changes and trends in providing relevant services to your client base. In evaluating these changes and trends to relevant services to your clients, it becomes important that you understand that there are many different characteristics of social work practice settings in which significant services to the lives of your client base are provided. You will come to understand that some of the relevant services you provide to your clients are from locales that are either private and/or public practice settings and include services in specialty practice areas such as health care and the criminal/juvenile justice systems.

You will further learn during your advanced or second year that relevant services provided by the health care practice setting include a network of service delivery to clients that may include diagnosis, treatment, and rehabilitation. Other relevant services might include health maintenance and prevention that are delivered across the continuum of care in various settings. Robert and Springer (2007) suggest that the social work profession has been providing services to incarcerated individuals since its inception in 1904 and is an essential component of the criminal justice system in the United States.

As advanced or second year MSW students, you will further understand that relevant services provided by social workers in the criminal justice field include behavioral health and case management services.

You will learn methods and strategies that will enable you to focus on the changes and trends in providing relevant services to your clients. You will further your understanding of the trends that will allow you to realize the significance of services in practice contexts such as those relevant services to immigrants and different religious/spiritual sects. During your academic training as a MSW student, you will continue to discover, appraise, and attend to changes and trends that result in providing relevant services that respond to the contexts that shape practice within your field placements and later during your private practices.

PROVIDING LEADERSHIP IN PROMOTING CHANGE IN SERVICE DELIVERY AND PRACTICE

You will learn that service delivery has many definitions but can be seen as the relationships between policy makers, service providers, and your client base that encompass services and their supporting systems. As MSW student practitioners, you will learn several strategies for providing leadership in promoting change in the service delivery to your client base. These strategies might include determining the demand for services to the community that are corroborated by research and analysis, and identifying the nature of the service demands (Armon, Berry, & Duncan, 2004). You will also learn another strategy might be analyzing other relevant services within the community in an attempt to quantify levels of service that can be achieved within your network system.

During your advanced or second year, you will learn that providing leadership that promotes change in service practice to your clients includes understanding the different approaches to or methods of service practice. You will come to understand that approaches that respond to these frameworks are generally effective if they are underpinned by a systematic understanding of the context of practice. Additionally, effective methods or approaches to service practice include steps to promote positive political and social change, as well as methods that secure positive environments that benefit the service delivery to your clients. As advanced or second year MSW student practitioners, you will understand that the delivery of services is only part of the response to contexts that shape practice. Interventions aimed at livelihoods and social protections should be considered as approaches to strengthening institutional arrangements for the delivery of services to your clients.

PRACTICE CONTEXTUAL BEHAVIORS AND ASSESS OUTCOMES

This section will help further your understanding of the practice behaviors for the 2008 CSWE EPAS 2.1.9. *Respond to contexts that shape practice*: (1) continuously discover, appraise, and attend to changing locales, populations, and scientific and technological developments; (2) understand the emerging societal trends to provide relevant services; and (3) provide leadership in promoting sustainable changes in service delivery and practice to improve the quality of social services. Each question will test your application of the practice behaviors and your ability to think critically regarding their function. The questions are deliberately varied and randomly placed regarding the three critical thinking practice behaviors.

Multiple Choice

(Note: On the lines below each multiple-choice question, explain why you chose that particular answer.)

Difficulty Scale: ✶ = Easy   ✶ ✶ = Moderate   ✶ ✶ ✶ = Challenging

1. Timothy is a second year MSW student interning at Cooper Counseling Center and has on his caseload seven-year-old Belinda, who has been physically abused by her mother, Linda. In play therapy, Timothy observes that Belinda acts out a violent situation with her toys. Timothy believes that her actions during the play therapy session may signal that Belinda's anger is beginning to surface. To verify his understanding of Belinda's feelings, the most appropriate step for Timothy to make is to:

    a. Use simple language, interpret Belinda's behavior, and assess her reaction.
    b. Prompt Belinda to talk about the game she played.
    c. Kindly ask the girl why her game is angry today.
    d. Ask her mother, Linda, to observe Belinda carefully from a position on the floor beside her as she plays another game using the same toys but in a less controlled environment, such has their home.

    Difficulty: ✶ ✶ = Moderate
    Topic: Discovering changes and trends to provide relevant services
    Practice Behavior: Discovering, appraising, and attending to changes and trends to provide relevant services

    _____

    _____

2. Denise is a medical social work intern in her final semester at a local public hospital in your county. Her patient Sammie informs her that she has made plans to commit suicide but asks Denise not to share her plans with anyone. The most inappropriate thing for Denise to do regarding service delivery to Sammie would be to:

    a. Document the conversation in Sammie's progress notes.
    b. Inform her immediate agency supervisor.
    c. Go along with Sammie's request and not share her information with anyone.

d. Document the conversation in Sammie's medical record.

Difficulty: ✳ = Easy
Topic: Appraising changes and trends to provide relevant services
Practice Behavior: Discovering, appraising, and attending to changes and trends to provide relevant services

_____

_____

3. You are in your first semester of your second year interning at a large chain department store in its employee assistance program. Morris, a young employee, has comes to you reporting that he has been experimenting with drugs and has recently come to work several times under the influence of meth. His supervisor Joan, who is a good friend of his, has clearly advised him that unless he receives some counseling, he will lose his job. Morris has severe feelings of guilt and shame concerning his mother, who "always tries to lead him down the right path." He states that his supervisor reminds him of his mother. As the employee assistance social worker, you first:

a. Refer Morris to a support group for meth addiction.
b. Assist Morris in finding new employment.
c. Deal with the ultimatum handed down by Morris's supervisor Joan regarding counseling.
d. Explore with Morris the dynamics of his relationship with his mother.

Difficulty: ✳ ✳ = Moderate
Topic: Promoting change in service practice
Practice Behavior: Providing leadership in promoting change in service delivery and practice

_____

_____

4. David, a MSW intern at a local social service agency, has a client, Annie, who states that she wants to discuss something that she did wrong. What should David tell Annie about confidentiality?

a. Tell Annie that everything is confidential under the privileged communication status.
b. Tell Annie that unless it is a danger to herself or others, it will be confidential.
c. Refer Annie to the agency lawyer for advice concerning the statute of limitations.

d. Nothing; wait to see if it's going to be a problem before addressing the issue.

Difficulty: ✲ = Easy

Topic: Appraising changes and trends to provide relevant services

Practice Behavior: Discovering, appraising, and attending to changes and trends to provide relevant services

_____

_____

5. Alexia is in her advanced year of her MSW program. To discover and appraise the culture of the new agency with which she is interning, she is attempting to determine the relationship between the environment variables and the patient's problem. The most appropriate method that will empower her to do so would be for Alexia to:

   a. Receive input from staff.
   b. Research the client's presenting problem.
   c. Obtain a complete comprehensive psychosocial history of the client.
   d. Plan and assess the tentative goals.

Difficulty: ✲ ✲ = Moderate

Topic: Appraising changes and trends to provide relevant services

Practice Behavior: Discovering, appraising, and attending to changes and trends to provide relevant services

_____

_____

6. You are interning as a crisis intervention counselor at a suicide hotline. You receive a call from a person who identifies himself as Jeffrey, who tells you that he is going to kill himself. To provide Jeffrey with the most relevant services due to him, you should first:

   a. Find out Jeffrey's location.
   b. Clarify how serious Jeffrey is regarding his desire to commit suicide.
   c. Ask if Jeffrey if he is alone or with someone.
   d. Establish rapport with Jeffrey in an attempt to get him to trust you.

Difficulty: ✲ = Easy

Topic: Providing leadership in promoting change in service delivery

Practice Behavior: Providing leadership in promoting change in service delivery and practice

_____

_____

7. Eli, a second year MSW student, is interning at You Must Live Counseling. He is preparing for the first session with a number of clients who are very depressed because of issues with their families, drugs, and the downward spiral of the economy. Eli's main concern in these initial interviews is to:

   a. Assess for the need to refer for a psychiatric diagnosis.
   b. Formulate the correct diagnosis for each client.
   c. Select the best medication for the clients depressed because of drug usage.
   d. Determine suicide intent.

   Difficulty: ✦✦✦ = Challenging
   Topic: Appraising changes and trends to provide relevant services
   Practice Behavior: Discovering, appraising, and attending to changes and trends to provide relevant services

   _____

   _____

8. Victor is interning as a school social worker at a Christian school in your area. While setting up a tutor for fifteen-year-old J. P., he learns that she is pregnant. J. P. has always been a good student of good moral fiber, so Victor obtains services for child care for her and WIC (Woman, Infant and Children) benefits in addition to her tutoring service. J. P. is still planning to drop out of school. What should Victor's next step be?

   a. Refer J. P. for alternative education.
   b. Obtain parent education for J. P.
   c. Let J. P. take leave for a semester.
   d. Explore J. P.'s decision to drop out of school.

   Difficulty: ✦✦ = Moderate
   Topic: Promoting change in service practice
   Practice Behavior: Providing leadership in promoting change in service delivery and practice

   _____

   _____

9. Paula, a second year MSW intern at Call Us Counseling Center, has been told by her client Stan during a therapy session that he intends to harm his girlfriend Whitney. He states that he has purchased a gun and will kill her when she returns to their apartment later that evening. Paula's responsibility as a social worker is to:

   a. Keep confidential all the information that Stan has shared with her.
   b. Inform Whitney of Stan's intention to do harm to her.

c. Call the police.
d. Document what Stan said and the advice given.

Difficulty: ✲ = Easy
Topic: Providing leadership in promoting change in service delivery
Practice Behavior: Providing leadership in promoting change in service delivery and practice

___

___

10. Johnny is in his last semester of his MSW program and is interning at the local community services board (CSB) in your county. He has been offered a full-time job with the CSB after graduation. He learns that the CSB has both billed Medicaid and received full payment from several clients. Johnny is troubled by this but is unsure as to whether it is merely an oversight or a calculated fraudulent act. The best strategy for Johnny to take is to:

a. Organize a group of workers and confront the director and the board.
b. Notify the appropriate state authorities and suggest an investigation.
c. Inform the executive director of the problem.
d. Contact the insurers and indicate that the CSB is billing inaccurately.

Difficulty: ✲✲✲ = Challenging
Topic: Providing leadership in promoting change in service practice
Practice Behavior: Providing leadership in promoting change in service delivery and practice

___

___

Essay Questions

1. Discuss two methods through which you can begin to discover changes and trends to provide relevant services to your clients at your field agency placements.
2. Discuss ways in which you can begin to attend to or concentrate on changes and trends that allow you to provide relevant services to your client base in your perspective field agencies and ultimately in your postgraduate practices.
3. Identify some private or public settings in which you have worked and discuss how you feel they will aid you in the shaping of your professional practice after graduation.
4. Discuss at least one technique through which you can begin to appraise or determine changes and trends to provide relevant services to your clients at your field agency placements.

Role-Play Exercise: "I Know What Happened to Me and I'm Concerned!"

Actions and responses to the role-play "I Know What Happened to Me and I'm Concerned!" will vary and depend on your individual characteristics, personal experience, and professional knowledge and are from your own perspective. Learn and enjoy!

You are a second year MSW student intern working at an adoption agency. You are a member of an ethnic minority and a product of the foster care system, as well. You have strong feelings regarding interracial adoptions and the negative impact they leave on families, particularly the children adopted into the families.

You are asked to facilitate an adoption in which a nonminority couple is seeking to adopt a minority child.

Consider the following scenarios in your role-play:

Scenario #1—You are struggling with your decision to continue to work with this family regarding the adoption and are sharing your concerns in the class and discussing it with a group of cohorts from your ethnic background.

Scenario #2—You are discussing your feelings, but with some reservations, with your agency supervisor, who is not from your ethnic background and is in fact very culturally incompetent

All participants must role-play how they would go about critically thinking about what they would do in this situation to demonstrate their ability to discover, appraise, and attend to changes and trends to provide relevant service delivery and practice.

Practice with MySocialWorkLab

Visit **MySocialWorkLab** at www.mysocialworklab.com to watch these competency-based videos.

Watch

Practice Context—**Keeping Up With Shifting Contexts**

Practice Context—**Attending to Changes and Relevant Services**

Practice Context—**Providing Leadership to Promote Change to Improve Quality of Social Services**

References

Armon, J., Berry, C., & Duncan, D. (2004). Service delivery in difficult environments; the case of Nepal. DFID, London. Retrieved June 16, 2011, from *http://www.grc-dfid.org.uk/grc/docs/EB96.pdf*

Robert, A., & Springer, D. (2007). *Social work in juvenile and criminal justice settings* (3rd Ed.). Springfield, IL: Charles C. Thomas.

10

ENGAGE, ASSESS, INTERVENE, EVALUATE

CSWE EPAS 2.1.10*(a)–(d) Engage, assess, intervene, and evaluate with individuals, families, groups, organizations, and communities*

Engage, assess, intervene, and evaluate are the tenth and final core competency of the 2008 EPAS and assimilate an integral degree of necessary knowledge, values, and skills that present a secure groundwork to build upon as an advanced or second year social work students. From these sets of core competencies, you will further your understanding of the different methods and collaborative processes by which to increase your knowledge and practice skills with individuals, families, groups, organizations, and communities. Moreover, you will learn that the various dimensions involved in the professional practice of social work include your recognizing, examining, and executing evidence-based interventions that are designed to achieve certain client goals.

You will be educated to understand the different techniques to employ when utilizing research and scientific improvements to evaluate program outcomes and measure practice effectiveness. In your advanced or second year, you will continue to recognize as well as communicate an understanding of the importance of developing, analyzing, and advocating for policies that benefit your clients and learn how to provide leadership that shapes policies and services (EPAS, 2008). During your final year in your perspective MSW programs, you will further your awareness of the need to promote social and economic justice.

As an advanced or second year practitioner student, you will understand the value of engagement and the techniques to effectively prepare for action with individuals, families, groups, organizations, and communities. You will further understand the assessment process as you learn to collect, organize, and interpret clients' data as well as evaluate their strengths and limitations. You will learn many techniques regarding intervention, some of which include initiating actions to achieve organizational goals; implementing prevention interventions that enhance client capacities, and negotiating, mediating, and advocating for your client population. During your final year as MSW students, you will develop an advanced understanding of evaluation as you critically analyze, monitor, and evaluate interventions (EPAS, 2008). These operational practice behaviors will serve as steps that will bridge your understanding to provide you with the tools to engage with, assess, intervene for, and evaluate individuals, families, groups, organizations, and communities.

You'll better understand how to prepare to work with your clients after securing an understanding of the types of services that you are able to provide through your agency, such as child welfare services, protective services for an abused child, foster care services for a child who has been orphaned because of the sudden death of his or her parents, or adoptions or services to unmarried parents. You will better prepare for action with individuals, families, groups, organizations and communities once you have gained a degree of understanding of your roles and how you navigate in and out of them; and gain a comfortable level of clarity regarding the practice settings where you will be working and providing services for your client base.

Using Empathy and Other Interpersonal Skills

As a foundation MSW student, you learned the importance of utilizing empathy with your clients and the impact that it can make when used properly. Being able to put aside your self-centered focus and view situations from another's perspective opens the way to empathy regarding your clients and (1) produces effective listening and (2) leads to more caring and compassion. As advanced or second year MSW students, you will further your understanding of the importance of interpersonal or social skills in professional practice. You will learn that good interpersonal skills enable you to interact respectfully with your professors, engage meaningfully with your cohorts, and communicate effectively with your field agency staff as well as with your client base and are vital for efficient, successful social work practice. During your advanced or second year, you will learn that the results of good interpersonal skills are oftentimes seen in your decision making, your self-confidence, your ability to work within a team setting or group, and your ability to collaborate with agencies or organizations within your community or network.

Developing a Mutually Agreed-On Focus of Work and Outcomes

In your first year of your MSW program, you learned different theories of human behavior that will assist you in working with your clients, such as (1) Sigmund Freud's psychoanalytic theory; (2) Erik Erikson's psycho-social stages of development; and (3) Piaget's theory of cognitive development. However, as advanced or second year MSW students, you'll further your understanding of these theoretical frameworks as you apply resources. them within the context of your field practice in developing a mutually agreed-on focus of work and outcomes with your clients. Many of the aforementioned theories will assist you; however, Piaget's theory of cognitive development is one that will help you cultivate a communally established focus of work for your clients and results for their efforts.

You will come to understand that the concepts for Piaget's intellectual development are action and operation. *Action* is the overt behavior of your clients; while *operation* is the particular kind of action that may be their internalized thoughts. The stages of cognitive development cover the life span of your client population and include (1) sensorimotor stage or infancy; (2) pre-operational stage or toddler and early childhood; (3) concrete operational stage or elementary and early adolescence; and (4) formal operational stage or adolescence and adulthood (Rogers, 2006; Schriver, 2011) During your advanced or second year, you will also begin to utilize cognitive-behavioral therapy when working with your clients, with an understanding that it is based on the idea that thoughts cause feelings and behaviors and that you can assist your client in changing the way he or she thinks, in order to feel and act better even if the situation does not change.

ASSESSMENT

During your foundation year, you possibly confused assessment with evaluation but came to understand the importance of the assessment process in recognizing the knowledge and skills set needed to practice as a professional social worker. As an advanced or second year MSW student, you will learn various practice approaches that include the assessment process. You will assess individuals, families, groups, organizations, and communities by understanding the different approaches to the assessment process in practice, such as the psychodynamic theory-based approach, the problem-solving approach, and the crisis intervention approach.

In the *psychodynamic theory-based approach,* assessment addresses (1) the "why" and "how" of the client's problem; (2) the shape of the current problem; and (3) the client's social and emotional resources (Rogers, 2006). The basic assessment of the *problem-solving approach* focuses first on problem identification and those aspects of the person-in-environment that can be engaged in problem solving. The assessment approach to *crisis intervention* explores the stress-producing event or situation; examines the individual's response to it; and examines the individual's responses to crises in the recent past (Schriver, 2011). As second year or advanced MSW student practitioners, your understanding of and familiarity with these approaches, as well as others, will better assist you in the assessment of individuals, families, groups, organizations, and communities within your client base.

ENGAGEMENT

During your advanced or second year in your perspective programs, you will further your understanding of the engagement process within your professional practice. In your perspective MSW programs, you will learn that there are several areas of understanding regarding the engagement process with your clients that can lend themselves to Actions of Professional Social Work Engagement (APSWE) that encompasses interactive processes including the application of critical thinking skills to complex client issues. You will come to comprehend these areas of APSWE to include: (1) your engagement in ongoing assessment of the existing conditions and circumstances of your client base; (2) your willingness to interface and create relationships within your client's family network in an effort to reach the designed practice goal; and (3) your desire to build connections and foster collaboration between communities with the particular issues, concerns, and needs of your client base. You will learn that by facilitating this engagement process, you will more effectively bridge the gaps between the services delivery and services utilization to your clients.

Preparing for Action with Individuals, Families, Groups, Organizations, and Communities

Much of your academic training in the classroom during your foundation year, your interaction with your cohorts during "in-class exercises" and assigned group projects, and your work at your perspective practicums with agency personnel have prepared you for actions with you clients during your advanced or second year as an MSW student. During your foundation year, you learned that in order to understand your clients within the context of their social and physical environment, you need to understand your role in service delivery to them. During your advanced or second year, you will gain more clarity with regard to the multiplicity of your identities as a social work clinician and the diversity of roles and responsibilities toward your client base. As an advanced social work student practitioner, you will further identify with various roles, including those of an advocate and educator or an organizer and a mediator.

As an advocate, you will learn steps to assisting your client in fighting for his or her rights as well as the rights of others to obtain needed resources.

Collecting, Organizing, and Interpreting Client Data

During the first year of your MSW program, you learned about direct service and system change strategies such as collecting and managing client data and methods for finding, assessing, and utilizing resources. However, during your advanced or second year, you will learn the importance of collecting, organizing, and interpreting client data. In order to engage with your clients, you must have some methods by which to collect or gather information on them. You will come to learn that methods of data collection and management include: (1) compiling specialized resource notebooks (hard copy) or electronic files on your computer, laptop, or agency iPad (e-Copy); (2) interviewing clients face-to-face, by phone, or via Internet such as on Skype; and/or (3) researching, such as by reading case files or through observation.

In order to assess client behaviors, you must have a system in place to organize client data, such as implementing an action plan of service delivery to your client, with a periodic review of the action plan to ensure accuracy of data. Lastly, in order to intervene on your client's behalf and evaluate behavior; you must have a method of interpreting data. As MSW students, you will observe firsthand that accurately evaluating your client can build trust within the professional relationship that communicates warmth, concern, and empathy, as well as knowledge, throughout your professional interactions with your client base.

Assessing Client Strengths and Limitations

As early as you can remember in your studies, you possibly can recall hearing that clients' strengths are central to the helping relationship and serve as an essential component of your practice with them. During your practice coursework in your foundation year, you learned the value in clients' strength as you learned about and became familiar with the strengths perspective of social work practice. You learned that the strengths perspective means that the strengths and resources to solve a problem lie within the client's interpersonal skills and emphasizes your clients' abilities, aptitudes, and skills to resolve issues. However, during your advanced or second year as MSW students, you will come to understand the importance of assessing client strengths when designing interventions to help resolve some of their problems and issues.

To help in assessing client strengths, Cowger (2004) identified twelve practice guidelines that foster a strengths perspective, two of which include: the ability to give pre-eminence to (1) the client's understanding of the facts; and (2) the ability to make assessment of strengths multidimensional. Even though your ability to assess clients' strengths depend on your practice situation and professional judgment, you will learn that doing so is invaluable in the empowerment of clients. As an advanced or second year MSW student, you will learn that assessing client limitations is equally important as assessing their strengths, particularly when engaging clients in designing interventions such as (1) obstacles to a true baseline related to time constraints and (2) building rapport with clients and gaining parental consent.

Developing Mutually Agreed-on Intervention Goals and Objectives

During your advanced or second year as MSW students, you will learn that some techniques for cultivating commonly established efforts regarding interventions goals and objectives with your client base include: (1) good practices in social service delivery; and (2) less intrusive service delivery models that engage clients in problem-solving efforts designed to build upon their strengths. You will learn many different models of service delivery in your perspective MSW programs. One model that will aid you in understanding steps to developing mutually agreed-on intervention goals and objectives of your client base is the integrated service delivery model (ISDM). The *integrated service delivery model* is a team-based, client-focused, service-centered approach to providing health and social services to clients, with a focus on integration and collaboration (ISDM, 2004). The three fundamental components of the integrated service delivery model include (1) utilization of the primary community care approach; (2) the need to ensure all clients and their organizations are interconnected; and (3) providing a clear service description as well as the need to strengthen core services (ISDM, 2004).

Selecting Appropriate Intervention Strategies

In the first year of your perspective MSW programs, you developed an understanding of the need for intervention strategies with your clients, as individuals, families, groups, communities, or organizations. You also learned that interventions were needed in order to assist your clients with solving their problems, resolving their issues, and alleviating the concerns impeding their pursuit of happiness. However, during your MSW program, you will learn processes by which to select appropriate intervention strategies for your clients. The interventions that you select with them depend on a variety of variables, such as the type of setting that you are working in, including hospitals, schools, prisons, or faith-based organizations.

Selecting appropriate intervention strategies also depends on the population that you are serving, such as children and youth, people with disabilities, or older adults, and the needs of your client, such as someone who has warning signs for anorexia nervosa and bulimia, or an abused child who needs protection from an abusive, addictive parent. You will also learn that when selecting appropriate interventions, you must be mindful of the cultural background of your clients. During your advanced or second year in your perspective MSW programs, you will learn that selecting appropriate intervention strategies for your clients is a process in which many considerations must be investigated, researched, and reviewed.

INTERVENTION

Initiating Actions to Achieve Organizational Goals

During your foundation year, you learned that the delivery of social work services can occur at many different levels and in various settings. Some of the levels at which you will practice are micro, mezzo, and macro. You learned that at the *micro* level, you initiate actions with individuals, families, and small groups, and at the *mezzo* level, you create teams with organizations and the network of helping professional agencies. At the *macro* level, you intervene with the community, institutions, and society when initiating action to achieve organizational goals with your client base. As MSW advanced or second year students, you will learn interventions that will enable you to initiate actions that will result in your achievement of the organizational goals of your internship agency.

The various settings in which you will initiate actions with your client include (1) governmental agencies, (2) nonprofit or voluntary organizations, and (3) the business sector. *Governmental agencies* provide services to the general public and operate within the parameters of the policies and procedures of law. They usually have organizational goals that meet the most basic needs of your client base, such as food, clothing, and shelter. You will learn that *nonprofit organizations* can have programs that are sectarian (faith-based) or non-sectarian. Examples of sectarian programs are those based in churches and synagogues, while non-sectarian programs also provide services to the public. The *business sector* can consist of private practice, such as your local social services agency or a large national for-profit organization.

Implementing Prevention Interventions, Enhancing Client Capacities

As an advanced or second year MSW student clinician, you'll learn how to work to assist clients in coping with unresolved difficulties in their lives; help them resolve current problems in their families; and promote awareness that prevents future problems. You will learn to implement prevention interventions that enhance their capacities to live up to their fullest potential. Morales, Sheafor, and Scott (2012) identified the three models of prevention as (1) primary, (2) secondary, and (3) tertiary. You will learn that *primary* prevention is when you try to change an environment by reducing or eliminating social, economic, and mental health conditions that contribute to client problems.

Secondary prevention is an issue that you identify that can be treated in a manner that keeps your client's situation from getting worse. *Tertiary* prevention is a situation that you, as the social worker, identify that helps your client cope with conditions that cannot be changed. During your advanced or second year, you will learn that the approaches to prevention interventions depend on a number of factors, such as the agency setting, the organizational mission, and goals—which will vary. However, some examples of approaches to implemented prevention interventions include a class action legal suit and combined court and community-based programs for prevention of juvenile delinquency (Morales, Sheafor & Scott, 2012).

Helping Resolve Client Problems

You learned early in your studies that one the main functions of social work is to empower clients to resolve problems. In helping resolve client problems, Morales, Sheafor, and Scott (2012) identify five fundamentals that fortify social work, two of which are (1) a commitment to social betterment and (2) an action orientation. They suggest that social betterment is more than just addressing problems, but improving certain aspects of the client's life that may surround the problem. Action orientation is doing something to prevent the problem, or helping a client to cope with the problem in the event that it cannot be changed.

The client is the center of social service delivery, and you will learn that there are a multiplicity of approaches to resolving client problems that depend on a number of factors, such as (1) your skill set and knowledge of the problem, (2) your clients' level of comprehension regarding the problem, (3) the degree to which you have influence over the source of the problem, and (4) the practice setting and the agency mission. Some examples of helping resolve clients' problems include (1) assisting clients to self-identify the services they need and want; (2) empowering clients to develop their own solutions to issues that are a priority for their family, based on intimate knowledge of it; and (3) modeling a method for resolving clients' problems using their own resources.

Negotiating, Mediating, and Advocating for Clients

During your MSW programs, you will learn of steps to adopt when negotiating, mediating, and advocating on behalf of your clients. The act of negotiating for your clients means making every attempt to bring together individuals, families, groups, and/or communities who are in conflict so that a bargain or compromise can be agreed upon and implemented on behalf of your clients. Advocating for your clients can mean many things but mainly that you assist in fighting for or securing their rights as well as the rights of others to obtain needed resources. You will learn that mediating for clients includes actions such as (1) intervening in disputes between parties in an effort to find compromises; (2) the reconciliation of differences; or (3) securing steps to reach agreements.

Facilitating Transitions and Endings

As advanced MSW student practitioners, you will learn to understand how to facilitate transitions and endings when engaging, assessing, intervening, and evaluating with individuals, families, groups, organizations, and communities. During the developmental stages of a professional relationship with your client base, you will learn steps to enable your clients to make the needed changes that will empower him or her to meet the goals of the service that you deliver to them to completion. To further understand how to facilitate transitions and endings regarding your client–social worker relationship, the National Association of Social Workers (NASW) Code of Ethics has identified several commonly held values: (1) respect and appreciation for individual and group differences; (2) commitment to developing clients' ability to help themselves; (3) willingness to transmit knowledge and skills to others; and (4) willingness to persist in efforts on behalf of clients despite frustration (NASW, 2008). During your final year in your perspective MSW program, you will learn to master an understanding of how to assist with needed changes and goal conclusions when engaging with, assessing, intervening for, and evaluating individuals, families, groups, organizations, and communities.

EVALUATION

Critically Analyzing, Monitoring, and Evaluating Interventions

During your advanced or second year, you will further your understanding of critically analyzing, monitoring, and evaluating interventions for your clients by identifying the knowledge and skills that are required for successful social work practice. You will learn that there are many "do's" or actions that you can adopt when critically analyzing, monitoring, and evaluating interventions on behalf of your clients; however, you will learn that there are some commonly known errors to avoid when undergoing this process. Some of these errors include: (1) overlooking client assets; (2) describing behavior unrelated to its context; (3) continuing intervention past its necessary time frame; (4) focusing upon irrelevant factors; (5) selecting ineffective intervention methods; and (6) withdrawing intervention too soon (Gambrill, 2009). When engaging with, assessing, intervening for, and evaluating individuals, families, groups, organizations, and communities, it is essential that you understand how to critically analyze, monitor, and evaluate interventions.

Practice Engagement, Assessment, Intervention, and Evaluation and Assess Outcomes

This section will help further your understanding of the practice behaviors for the 2008 CSWE EPAS 2.1.10(a)–(d) *Engage, assess, intervene, and evaluate with individuals, families, groups, organizations, and communities*. Your review of the following sixty-four questions and your understanding of the answers will better your abilities to (1) engage with your client base; (2) assess their needs; (3) designing interventions; and (4) evaluate the strategies you utilize in professional practice with individuals, families, groups, organizations, and communities. Each question will test your application of the practice behaviors and your ability to critically think regarding their function. The questions are deliberately varied and randomly placed regarding the four practice behaviors.

Multiple Choice

(Note: On the lines below each multiple-choice question, explain why you chose that particular answer.)

Difficulty Scale: ✳ = Easy   ✳ ✳ = Moderate   ✳ ✳ ✳ = Challenging

1. Dennis, a second year social work intern, is working with an agency that provides networking services to recently released sex offenders. He has worked considerably with Olivia, a fifty-three-year-old female, and has helped her to obtain employment. Olivia has been doing well on the job and has received positive evaluations from her supervisor, Mitchell. She is now requesting to terminate her work with Dennis and expresses her concerns about making it. What would be the best action for Dennis to take in addressing Olivia's concerns regarding her desire to terminate services?

   a. Dennis should listen to Olivia's concerns and solve her problems regarding the termination.
   b. Dennis should share that he can identify with Olivia and not terminate the services until they both feel that it is time to do so.
   c. Dennis should emphasize Olivia's role in changing her situation and express that he understands her concerns regarding her need to terminate but that perhaps it is time to do.
   d. Dennis should dismiss Olivia's concerns and terminate the services based upon her good performance.

   Difficulty: ✳ ✳ = Moderate
   Topic: Assessment
   Practice Behavior: Assessing client strengths and limitations

   _____

   _____

2. James, a second year MSW student has sought the advice of his agency supervisor, Evan, regarding some challenges he has faced facilitating the group "Heads Up," which he started. James has decided to terminate one of the group members, JJ, because he is continually disruptive during group and is hindering the growth of the group. The most appropriate advice for Evan to give James is:

   a. To tell JJ that he will see him individually to tell him what he needs to do in order to change his behavior.
   b. To tell "Heads Up" about the pending termination of JJ and deal with the response to the termination in the next several group sessions.

c. For James to tell the group "Heads Up" about the discussion with his supervisor Evan and elicit their feedback before he takes action to terminate JJ from the group.

d. To tell JJ that he will be terminated in four weeks regardless of what he says.

Difficulty: ✲✲ = Moderate

Topic: Evaluation

Practice Behavior: Critically analyzing, monitoring, and evaluating interventions

_____

_____

3. Carolina, a recent MSW graduate from the state university in your city, has been hired at her internship agency as a counselor. She has been working with Millie, an emotionally disturbed nineteen-year-old technologically advanced female, since she was placed in the agency and has felt that the treatment goals and plan need to be revised. What should be Carolina's next step in considering changes in Millie's treatment plan?

   a. Carolina should text Millie possible changes to the treatment plan and discuss them with her parents only after Millie has approved them.

   b. Carolina should discuss the needed changes to Millie's treatment plan with Millie's parents before discussing them with Millie.

   c. Carolina should conduct a session with Millie and her parents and introduce the suggested changes with them for their approval.

   d. Carolina should first discuss the changes with Millie, secure her approval, and then present them to Millie's parents with her approval.

Difficulty: ✲✲ = Moderate

Topic: Engagement

Practice Behavior: Preparing for action with individuals, families, groups, organizations, and communities

_____

_____

4. Selma is an MSW student intern in her second year. She is working for a local advocacy agency and has been selected as the leader of a task group that will organize the next lobby day. What is the most appropriate next step for Selma to take?

   a. Selma should carefully plan and then facilitate the task group meetings.

b. Selma should allow the group members to individually plan the next meetings but take responsibility for facilitating the meetings.

c. Selma should assign some meeting planning and coordination tasks to members of the task group.

d. Selma should totally avoid influencing the task group's processes.

Difficulty: ✳✳✳ = Challenging
Topic: Engagement
Practice Behavior: Preparing for action with organizations

---

5. James, an MSW student intern, is working at a local social service agency and has collaborated with his agency supervisor regarding terminating his client JJ from his caseload. When considering the process of termination, the most inappropriate intervention would be for:

a. James to evaluate the accomplished goals with JJ before termination.

b. James to discuss with JJ his sense of loss regarding the termination.

c. James to establish outcome objectives with JJ.

d. James to discuss his feelings regarding termination.

Difficulty: ✳ = Easy
Topic: Intervention
Practice Behavior: Facilitating transitions and endings

---

6. William is an advanced MSW student interning as a school social worker at one of the local middle schools in your area. Pamela, a twelve-year-old female student, is sent to William's office because of complaints of her "acting out" in class and excessive unexcused absences. Pamela reveals that at home she is oftentimes left alone without food, scared. She states that her father works during the day at the shoe factory and sells drugs most nights. How can William best help Pamela?

a. Pamela needs help in defending herself against drugs and should receive counseling focused on self-defense.

b. William should call the police to report Pamela's father's illegal drug activities.

   c. William should discuss Pamela's situation with the field director at his school and seek guidance in developing a comprehensive strategy for Pamela and her father.

   d. William must react to the information learned from Pamela and report his concerns to his agency supervisor, which will result in a report being filed with the local child protective agency.

Difficulty: ✳✳ = Moderate

Topic: Engagement

Practice Behavior: Preparing for action with individuals, families, groups, organizations, and communities

_____

_____

7. Crosby, a second year MSW student, is facilitating a weekly group at a local men's shelter. Milton, one of the group members, is upset and is planning to leave the group because of unresolved differences with Vincent, another group member. Of the following possible responses, Crosby should least likely:

   a. Suggest that he facilitate a meeting between Milton and Vincent prior to any final decision being made regarding Milton leaving the group.

   b. Recommend that the members discuss their feelings regarding Milton leaving the group.

   c. Suggest that Milton review the progress made on his objectives.

   d. Suggest that the group members ignore the fact that Milton is leaving the group.

Difficulty: ✳✳ = Moderate

Topic: Engagement

Practice Behavior: Preparing for action with individuals, families, groups, organizations, and communities

_____

_____

8. Tex is in his final semester as a school social work intern at one of the elementary schools in his local community. He receives a referral from one of the recently hired third-grade teachers that an eight-year-old boy named PJ is extremely withdrawn and poorly dressed in her class. Tex will first:

   a. Refer PJ to a child psychologist.

   b. Call PJ's parents to investigate the problem.

c. Observe PJ in class.

d. Set up an interview with PJ.

Difficulty: ✶✶ = Easy

Topic: Assessment

Practice Behavior: Collecting, organizing, and interpreting client data

_____

_____

9. Dennis is an MSW intern in his final week at a social service agency. He has provided a number of marital sessions to Carlton and Terri, a couple with a history of sexual and drug abuse. Carlton has been out of the house for a number of months; however, Terri wants him to come back and requests that Dennis conduct an individual session with Carlton to encourage him to come home. The most appropriate step is for:

a. Dennis to refuse to schedule an individual session with Carlton.

b. Dennis to do nothing and ignore Terri's request.

c. Dennis to share with Terri his role as a counselor and wait for Carlton to schedule an appointment for individual marital counseling.

d. Dennis to plan to conduct the individual session with Carlton and demand that he reunite with his wife, Terri.

Difficulty: ✶✶ ✶✶ = Moderate

Topic: Intervention

Practice Behavior: Implementing prevention interventions, enhancing client capacities

_____

_____

10. Austin, a second year MSW medical social work student, is interning at Mountain View Public Hospital. His client Beverly tells Austin that her cousin Peter is taking her prescribed medication for personal use. The most appropriate action for Austin to take is:

a. To report the incident to the psychiatrist for possible changes in meds.

b. To call the police and report it.

c. To document the incident and notify the hospital staff.

d. To demand that Beverly provide his home address and confront Peter about his illegal use of her prescription drugs.

Difficulty: ✦ = Easy
Topic: Intervention
Practice Behavior: Initiating actions to achieve organizational goals

---

11. Evan, a recent MSW graduate, is working with a private agency that provides wraparound services to the local juvenile court system. The court has referred a group of adolescent members from different gangs to Evan for group counseling. He attempts to use the same group methods that he utilized with a voluntary group of adult gang members with the adolescent gang members ordered into counseling by the court, but he has been unsuccessful. The most probable reason for the lack of success is that:

    a. Evan did not follow the proper intake and contracting procedures with the adolescent group.
    b. The adolescent gang group are involuntary clients mandated by the courts and are resisting the service.
    c. Delinquent adolescent clients do not normally respond to group programs.
    d. The group members have no prior relationships with each other and feel estranged.

Difficulty: ✦ ✦ = Moderate
Topic: Engagement
Practice Behavior: Preparing for action with individuals, families, groups, organizations, and communities

---

12. Joan, an LMSW at Helping Hands, is counseling Gloria, a married woman struggling with her husband's addiction to video and electronic games (gaming). She complains that George is inattentive to her physical needs. She also complains that George has, on several occasions, spent days playing an Internet tournament, which affected his job negatively and her indirectly. The conversations of the sessions with Gloria seem to always emphasize George's behavior. Joan should:

    a. Determine with Gloria if both she and her husband are the clients.
    b. Have Gloria call Gamers Anonymous.

c. Ask Gloria that her husband come in for an individual session.

d. Refer Gloria to a counselor who specializes in gaming addictions.

Difficulty: ✲ ✲ = Moderate

Topic: Engagement

Practice Behavior: Preparing for action with individuals, families, groups, organizations, and communities

---

13. Anita, a second year MSW student intern, has been placed at the local convalescent home in your community since the beginning of her first year in her MSW program. She has worked with her favorite group of senior citizens for months and has noticed a pattern of interaction that oftentimes results in arguments between several of the senior citizens, with final outcomes that hinder the growth of the group. The most appropriate step in this situation is for:

a. Anita to speak to the committee leader after the meeting.

b. Anita to turn the problem over to the group and focus on alternative ways to advance the committee's agenda.

c. Anita to concentrate on the contract upon which they previously agreed.

d. Anita to emphasize that the quarrelling impedes the development of trust and intimacy.

Difficulty: ✲ = Easy

Topic: Engagement

Practice Behavior: Using empathy and other interpersonal skills

---

14. Gina, a second year MSW student, is interning at a social service agency that specializes in counseling interracial couples. She is in the initial phase of treatment for Tina and Thomas T. The primary task for Gina regarding this particular phase of treatment is for:

a. Gina to gather information for a psychosocial diagnosis both for Tina and Thomas T.

b. Gina to engage Tina and Thomas T. in treatment.

c. Gina to establish a relationship with Tina and Thomas T.

d. Gina to understand why Tina and Thomas T. are seeking help.

Difficulty: ✵ = Easy

Topic: Engagement

Practice Behavior: Developing a mutually agreed-on focus of work and outcomes

_____

_____

15. Glen, a second year MSW student, is interning at Families Forever, a social service agency that partners with the local juvenile courts in providing wraparound services to at-risk youth. Marco, age fifteen, and Trina, age fourteen, are mandated for treatment with Families Forever because of serious issues with lack of respect for their parents, adults, and people of power. During the initial session with Marco and Trina, Glenn should reasonably expect that there will be a need to:

a. Focus on the issue of race of the worker.

b. Focus on the issue of authority.

c. Focus on the issue of the setting of the meetings.

d. Focus on the issue of confidentiality.

Difficulty: ✵ = Easy

Topic: Assessment

Practice Behavior: Collecting, organizing, and interpreting client data

_____

_____

16. Rose is in her first year at a local state university and has experimented with marijuana since her sophomore year in high school. In an attempt to change her life, she is seeking treatment both at the university counseling center and with an off-campus social service agency. Rose has been able to move off campus into her own apartment and lives alone because she has been unable to find a roommate. She has income as of a result of receiving Supplemental Security Income (SSI) because of her severe depression. Rose has been subscribed medication for her depression; however, she complains to her social worker that she still experiences strong emotions. She constantly has thoughts of worthlessness and loneliness and wonders why she is still alive. Michelle is the social work intern assigned to work with Rose. Under these circumstances, the social worker would be most concerned about:

a. The need for Rose to have recreational outlets.

b. Rose securing employment that will result in her having a more responsible and rewarding means of earning an income.

c. The possibility that Rose might attempt suicide.

   d. Rose's unmet medical needs.

Difficulty: ⁂ = Easy

Topic: Assessment

Practice Behavior: Selecting appropriate intervention strategies

_____

_____

17. Vanessa, a second year MSW student, is facilitating a group on trust and respect with eight adolescent girls at the local community services board. Three of the group members, Josie, Annie, and Bonnie, want to discuss something about another group member and call Vanessa asking for an individual session. The most appropriate action to take is for:

   a. Vanessa to ask Josie, Annie, and Bonnie to bring up their concerns at the next group session.

   b. Vanessa to express her disappointment at the lack of trust and respect that Josie, Annie, and Bonnie have displayed.

   c. Vanessa to give an appointment for an individual session only to Josie, because she was the spokesperson for the trio, and conduct the session before the group meets again.

   d. Vanessa to refer Josie, Annie, and Bonnie to another counselor who is not as involved as she.

Difficulty: ⁂ = Easy

Topic: Engagement

Practice Behavior: Preparing for action with individuals, families, groups, organizations, and communities

_____

_____

18. Eighteen-year-old Brenda is in the eighth month of her pregnancy and has decided, with the encouragement of her parents, to give her baby up for adoption; however, she refuses to reveal the name of the child's father. In doing so, she has put at risk the legal adoption of her unborn child because of the need for the father's approval and background of his health history. You are the social worker assigned to this case. You should:

   a. Decide first to deny Brenda service until she provides this information to the proper parties.

   b. Attempt to help Brenda to understand the value of giving this information to the adoption agency.

c. Ask the court to mandate that Brenda disclose this information in the interest of the unborn child.

   d. Attempt to obtain this information through interviews with the parents or close friends of Brenda's and through Facebook and other social media.

Difficulty: ✻ ✻ = Moderate

Topic: Assessment

Practice Behavior: Collecting, organizing, and interpreting client data

_____

_____

19. Richard is in his final year as an MSW intern at Third Chance Counseling (TCC), a drug and substance abuse treatment agency, and has Connie on his caseload. Connie complains that two of the health care professionals at TCC have never liked her and oftentimes misunderstood her. In such a situation the first and best assessment is that:

   a. Richard should acknowledge that Connie's concerns are a common problem, because he, too, has had similar concerns, in an effort to minimize her anxiety.

   b. Richard should consult with his agency supervisor about Connie's complaint and suggest that the other health care professionals handle their concerns individually with her.

   c. Richard should explore Connie's reasons for her feelings and offer to discuss them immediately with each health care professional on her behalf.

   d. Richard should explore with Connie the reasons for her feelings and help her discuss them directly with the two health care professionals.

Difficulty: ✻ ✻ = Moderate

Topic: Assessment

Practice Behavior: Collecting, organizing, and interpreting client data

_____

_____

20. Tim, a recent MSW graduate, is counseling Scott, who has just lost an infant child due to Sudden Infant Death Syndrome (SIDS). Tim tells Scott, "I remember what a painful experience I went through when I lost my child three months ago." Tim is best demonstrating:

   a. Empathy and a respect for Scott's autonomy.

    b. Modeling broad-mindedness by sharing his painful experience with the loss of his child.

    c. Permissiveness to vent pain as a means to better cope with loss.

    d. Self-disclosure and support for Scott's feelings.

Difficulty: ✷ = Easy

Topic: Engagement

Practice Behavior: Using empathy and other interpersonal skills

---

21. Drake, a second year MSW intern, is counseling PJ, who has mentioned a fantasy involving sexual activity with his teenage son. He shares that feels guilty about the thought and states he would never act on this fantasy. The most appropriate action is for:

    a. Drake to inform PJ that discussing this topic is not appropriate.

    b. Drake to notify the local child protective agency concerning possible sexual abuse.

    c. Drake to help PJ differentiate between responsibility for thoughts and actions and help him explore the basic roots of his thoughts.

    d. Drake to talk with PJ's son to assess if he has been inappropriately touched by his father.

Difficulty: ✷ ✷ ✷ = Challenging

Topic: Engagement

Practice Behavior: Preparing for action with individuals, families, groups, organizations, and communities

---

22. Between the ages of thirteen and twenty-one, CJ was addicted to pornography and marijuana; however, he has been drug-free since receiving your therapy. He has also reduced his addiction to pornography but is having serious relationship issues with his girlfriend and with his brother Troy, who first introduced him to pornography at the age of thirteen. His acquaintances with friends are short-lived and unproductive, and he loses his temper easily when frustrated. CJ also believes the managers at his place of employment are unfair and excessively critical. You might first suspect that:

    a. CJ's long period of addictions since adolescence has led to a failure to develop age-appropriate interpersonal skills.

    b. CJ's girlfriend and his brother needs help in accepting him back into the family.

c. CJ may have begun to use drugs again and is trying to hide his addiction to pornography by isolating himself from others.

d. CJ has a serious problem with authority that prevents him from following the orders of his employer and others assigned to delegate him duties.

Difficulty: ✲ ✲ = Moderate
Topic: Assessment
Practice Behavior: Assessing client strengths and limitations

_____

_____

23. Mark, age nineteen, has always had problems with his anger and has been in and out of Regional Youth Detention Centers (RYDC), but, until now, never to the point of involving him in the adult legal system. He has always managed to "bounce back" since the anger problem was noticed at the age of thirteen. His parents are finally fed up with Mark's behavior and refuse to get him out of trouble by signing their home as security for his bond. Glen, who has been the family social work counselor, should:

a. Support Mark's parents in their firmness, as this may help Mark to fully confront the damage he is doing to himself and his family, and motivate him to change.

b. Help Mark confront the situation that he now faces and assist him in finding the treatment resources he needs.

c. Advise his parents to relax their position and give Mark a chance to work on his anger management while out of jail, since there are no anger rehabilitative programs available for anyone while incarcerated.

d. Point out to Mark that if he is genuinely trying to change, he can persuade his parents to concede and sign his bond using their house as collateral.

Difficulty: ✲ ✲ = Moderate
Topic: Intervention
Practice Behavior: Helping resolve client problems

_____

_____

24. Brandon is an advanced MSW student in his first semester of his final year at a local social service agency. Although he received his BSW five years ago, he did not work in the field after graduation but worked as a real estate agent. Brandon is assigned his first client, Troy, but is somewhat nervous about how to professionally respond to Troy's needs. When working with Troy, the most appropriate approach for Brandon to employ is:

a. To accept Troy with positive though conditional regard.

b. To advocate moral responsibility to Troy—encourage him to always "do the right thing."

c. To accept Troy unconditionally.

d. To be open and permissive toward Troy.

Difficulty: ✸ = Easy

Topic: Assessment

Practice Behavior: Selecting appropriate intervention strategies

---

---

25. Zack is an advanced MSW student interning as a school social worker at one of the local high schools in your community, and Kirk is his client suffering from discrimination as a result of being one of the few minorities at the school. In an effort to demonstrate professional behavior toward his client:

a. Zack should show all feelings freely to foster spontaneous interaction with Kirk.

b. Zack should avoid fixed positions and pre-established attitudes about Kirk.

c. Zack should agree with Kirk in an effort to build confidence in the professional relationship.

d. Zack should remain impassive toward Kirk as a means to encourage the professional relationship.

Difficulty: ✸ ✸ = Moderate

Topic: Engagement

Practice Behavior: Preparing for action with individuals, families, groups, organizations, and communities

---

---

26. Carey, a MSW second year student, is interning at a group home for boys. He is very close in age to most of the group home residents and is oftentimes faced with challenges in gaining their respect. Scott, one of the group home residents, makes negative remarks about Carey and disagrees with him in group. Irritated and annoyed by this behavior, the best response is for Carey to:

a. Speak to Scott after the group meeting and tell him how he feels.

b. Do nothing until it happens again.

c. Allow the group to respond, since this is not typically the way group members communicate with one another.

d. Communicate the feelings of annoyance and suggest to Scott that there are more appropriate ways of communicating his disagreement with him.

Difficulty: ✵ = Easy
Topic: Engagement
Practice Behavior: Using empathy and other interpersonal skills

_____

_____

27. Zora, a recent MSW graduate, is in an agency that receives clients who are mandated by the courts for treatment. She is working with fifteen-year-old Dorothy regarding her defiance toward authority. Her family is very disengaged regarding treatment. Zora could suspect that the major problem that contributes to this disengaged behavior is most likely that:

a. There has been no bonding between Dorothy and her family.
b. Dorothy is acting out.
c. Dorothy's family is unable to make a commitment to her because of her defiance toward authority.
d. The family is so closely knit that they do not respond individually to treatment.

Difficulty: ✵ = Easy
Topic: Engagement
Practice Behavior: Preparing for action with individuals, families, groups, organizations, and communities

_____

_____

28. Tiffany is in her second semester of her advanced year as an MSW student. While interning at her placement, she has learned that a number of clients have exhibited hostile behavior toward the agency and spoken negatively about several of its key counselors and administrators. The first and most appropriate action to take is for:

a. Tiffany to express the agency viewpoint when hostile or negative attitudes are expressed by clients.
b. Tiffany to assume the clients have problems with authority.
c. Tiffany to help clients assess the extent to which their reactions are emotionally appropriate.

d. Tiffany to support clients' negative feelings about the agency, when agency policy is unreasonable.

Difficulty: ✳ = Easy

Topic: Intervention

Practice Behavior: Implementing prevention interventions, enhancing client capacities

_____

_____

29. A group of pre-teen males, whose fathers have recently been incarcerated, voluntarily meet at the local community center with Scott, a Licensed Master Social Worker (LMSW). The purpose of the group has been explained to the boys, and Scott has welcomed everyone. During the first moments of the meeting, the participants are silent. Scott, the social worker facilitating the group, might initially say:

a. Nothing.
b. "I do understand your silence, because the first meeting is always a difficult one."
c. "The group seems unusually quiet."
d. "The group was formed to help you think about your new situation. I wonder what you would like to talk about."

Difficulty: ✳ = Easy

Topic: Engagement

Practice Behavior: Using empathy and other interpersonal skills

_____

_____

30. Cody, a social worker at Helping, Inc., finds it possible to be effective only by relating in different ways to clients, on the one hand, and staff, on the other. Cody's change of attitude and conversational style in dealing with the very different groups is:

a. Inappropriate, because as an employee of Helping, Inc., Cody's first loyalty is to them.
b. Appropriate, because Cody need only respond to the client population and can be dishonest to the staff of Helping, Inc.
c. Appropriate, as there are conflicting pressures from each group, and Cody responds to both groups' concerns to remain effective.

d. Inappropriate, because professional ethics dictate that a social worker be consistent.

Difficulty: ✲✲ = Moderate

Topic: Engagement

Practice Behavior: Using empathy and other interpersonal skills

31. In developing an understanding of the basic behavior of her client Tim, Tiffany, a second year MSW intern student, should first:

a. Estimate when Tim is ready to both share and contribute to understanding his own behavior and then discuss it with her.
b. Direct Tim toward awareness without interpretation.
c. Continue to observe Tim by writing down his behaviors and discuss her notes during her Human Behavior and the Social Environment (HBSE) class.
d. Share all of her learned information with Tim.

Difficulty: ✲ = Easy

Topic: Engagement

Practice Behavior: Developing a mutually agreed-on focus of work and outcomes

32. Eva, a medical social worker at a psychiatric unit of a mental hospital, is treating Jennifer, who is diagnosed with a borderline condition. In the case of a borderline condition, it is generally recommended as her social worker that:

a. Eva should focus on the issue of dependency and Jennifer's inability to choose life goals.
b. Eva should confront Jennifer on the use of diminishing defenses.
c. Eva should allow Jennifer to feel in control of the session.
d. Eva should urge Jennifer to accept group treatment, preferably the Gestalt approach.

Difficulty: ✲ = Easy

Topic: Assessment

Practice Behavior: Developing a mutually agreed-on focus of work and outcomes

33. Jill is in her final year of her MSW program at Your University (YU) and is interning at the Hope Center as a geriatric social work student. During a counseling session, one of her favorite clients, Virginia, tells her that she is going to kill herself and then her husband, Virgil. Jill has conducted marital sessions with both Virginia and Virgil in the past and therefore has a professional working relationship with both of them. However, after careful evaluation of Virginia, Jill determines that the threat appears to reflect real intent rather than being ideational. The first action to take is for:

   a. Jill, the MSW intern, to talk with Virgil.
   b. Jill, the MSW intern, to speak with the field director at YU for advice on what to do.
   c. Jill, the social worker, should contact the police immediately.
   d. Jill, the social worker, should maintain the confidentiality of the communication with Virginia.

   Difficulty: ✲ ✲ = Moderate

   Topic: Engagement

   Practice Behavior: Preparing for action with individuals, families, groups, organizations, and communities

   _____

   _____

34. Social worker Tim is explaining informed consent to Virgil, a participant in a research project that is being conducting at his field agency. In explaining the concept of informed consent, the most appropriate statement would be for:

   a. Tim to explain to Virgil that informed consent gives him the right to know the purpose and nature of all aspects of his treatment in the research project.
   b. Tim to explain to Virgil that informed consent gives the right to his field director at his university to know the purpose and nature of all aspects of his treatment in the research project.
   c. Tim, as a social work student, must inform his field director of any severe client misconduct of any of the participants in the research project, including Virgil.
   d. Tim, as member of the social work profession, must inform NASW of any severe client misconduct of any of the participants in the research project, including Virgil.

   Difficulty: ✲ ✲ = Moderate

   Topic: Engagement

   Practice Behavior: Developing a mutually agreed-on focus of work and outcomes

   _____

   _____

35. Taylor, a non-minority MSW student intern, has been working in a predominantly African American and Latino community for eight months. During a discussion about local service agencies, two community members, Shawna and Maria, conveyed bitterness and some hostility toward Taylor and social workers "like her" working in minority communities. A few other members also questioned whether non-minority workers could be sensitive to clients' needs. The most appropriate action is for:

   a. Taylor to not respond to the expression of hostility by Shawna and Maria and simply express her own opinions.
   b. Taylor to not respond directly to Shawna and Maria's remarks and behavior; but to discuss their concerns with her field director at her university during the weekly integrative seminar.
   c. Taylor to express her true feelings in an effort to force Shawna and Maria to question and confront their own values and lack of sensitivity.
   d. Taylor to respond permissively to the issue raised by Shawna and Maria, while making her own values and attitudes clear to the community members.

   Difficulty: ✦✦ = Moderate

   Topic: Engagement

   Practice Behavior: Preparing for action with individuals, families, groups, organizations, and communities

   _____

   _____

36. Miranda has just graduated with her MSW and is working with MSW-PRN, an agency that provides social services contract employment with participating social service agencies in your state for new MSW graduates. In practicing the techniques of supportive therapy with her client Theresa, the most appropriate strategy is for:

   a. Miranda to give advice and help Theresa to deal with maladaptive coping.
   b. Miranda to allow Theresa to reveal and manage her own unconscious material by responding with empathy and understanding.
   c. Miranda to consciously avoid unleashing unconscious, repressed material and use clarification when working with Theresa.
   d. Miranda to encourage and give emotional support to Theresa in an effort to increase her self-esteem.

   Difficulty: ✦✦✦ = Challenging

   Topic: Assessment

   Practice Behavior: Developing mutually agreed-on intervention goals and objectives

   _____

   _____

37. Dawn, an advanced MSW student, is conducting an individual session with Julie. Julie has been married to Mark for fifteen years and reports that Mark has begun to lose interest in her. The best approach in this situation is for:

   a. Dawn to suggest to Julie that she and her husband, Mark, enter marital counseling.
   b. Dawn to encourage Julie to express her feelings.
   c. Dawn to share with Julie that given the number of years that she and Mark have been together, his behavior is normal.
   d. Dawn to reflect on Julie's issue as pathological, requiring remediation.

   Difficulty: ✸ = Easy
   Topic: Assessment
   Practice Behavior: Developing a mutually agreed-on focus of work and outcomes

   _____

   _____

38. Justin, an MSW intern, is working at a local social service agency in your county that provides anger management training to single parents accused of verbal and physical abuse of their children. Justin is trying to develop a treatment plan for Jada. Which is the most appropriate strategy regarding the development of his clinical relationship with Jada?

   a. Justin can rely on Jada to be more receptive, responsive and responsible.
   b. Justin can work more extensively and develop varied intervention and practical techniques for Jada.
   c. Justin can allow some familiarity to enter the relationship with Jada.
   d. Justin can expect greater equality in the relationship with Jada.

   Difficulty: ✸ ✸ = Moderate
   Topic: Assessment
   Practice Behavior: Developing mutually agreed-on intervention goals and objectives

   _____

   _____

39. Dalton, a second year MSW student, is working with fourteen-year-old James and his mother, Deidra. In selecting the most appropriate intervention strategies with James, the more successful technique in altering his personality in relation to his mother would be for:

a. Dalton to suggest behavior modification for James while working on the manipulation of his mother Deidra's environment.
b. Dalton to suggest the manipulation of James's environment while working on behavior modification with his mother, Deidra.
c. Dalton to suggest mirroring James's environment, while working on the manipulation of his mother Deidra's environment.
d. Dalton to utilize free association with James, while working on the manipulation of his mother Deidra's environment.

Difficulty: ☆ = Easy
Topic: Assessment
Practice Behavior: Selecting appropriate intervention strategies

40. Doug, an LMSW, is providing therapy to Lincoln. During a very challenging time, Lincoln, seriously upset, out of control, and suffering from chronic depression, voluntarily signs himself into an inpatient unit. After three hours, Lincoln decides to leave and refuses to consider a longer stay, even though Dallas, the LCSW at the hospital, recommended more inpatient treatment. The best option for the LMSW, Doug, is:

a. For both Doug and Dallas to seek a court order.
b. For Doug and Dallas to enlist Lincoln's family's aid to convince him to stay.
c. For Doug and Dallas to assist Lincoln with a plan for after-care living arrangements.
d. For Doug to recommend continued hospitalization despite Lincoln's wish to leave.

Difficulty: ☆☆= Easy
Topic: Intervention
Practice Behavior: Helping resolve client problems

41. A local church, concerned about the area health and education of its church community, employs Anita, a community social work advocate, to explore their problems further and develop new programs. Anita tries first to establish a relationship with a variety of community representatives and then involves herself in preliminary discussions about the problems with their state representative, Senator Bowles. After the local church has determined initial program objectives, the best option is for:

a. Anita, the social work advocate, to continue meeting with the local church and provide support for the activities they decide to participate in.
b. Anita to prepare a proposal that will enable the group to find funds to develop the programs she feels are necessary.
c. Anita to share all findings from Senator Bowles and advise the local church of the route they must take to meet their objectives.
d. Senator Bowles to plan the assigned tasks for the local church group.

Difficulty: ✻ ✻ ✻ = Challenging
Topic: Engagement
Practice Behavior: Preparing for action with individuals, families, groups, organizations, and communities

_____

_____

42. Nina is an advanced MSW student interning at the local Department of Family and Children Services (DFCS) in your county. She determines that thirteen-year-old Brianna is being physically abused; however, the parents deny that abuse has occurred. The first thing to be done is for:

a. Nina to avoid confronting the parents with her knowledge until she has a one-on-one with each parent.
b. Nina to try to improve Brianna's situation but keep the family intact in the process.
c. Nina to take necessary measures to provide for Brianna's safety.
d. Nina to work to get the parents to individually admit to their abuse of their thirteen-year-old daughter.

Difficulty: ✻ = Easy
Topic: Assessment
Practice Behavior: Selecting appropriate intervention strategies

_____

_____

43. Melody shares concerns with her social worker, Freda, that when her husband, Tony, comes home from his gambling trips at the casino, he is oftentimes verbally and physically aggressive with her and their children. Tony's weekend gambling excursions with his best friend, Linda, have increased, and it is clear to Melody that he is spending the

money they reserve to pay their household bills. He has refused to give her money for the rent and the groceries in the last month. Melody is noticeably fearful and asks Freda for assistance. What should the social worker do first?

a. Freda should work with Melody to help her protect herself and the children, and plan for alternative means to pay the rent and purchase groceries.

b. Freda should ask Tony to come in for counseling and work with him about his possible gambling problem.

c. Freda should suggest a mental examination for Melody and the children.

d. Freda should suggest family treatment to encourage Tony to seek help.

Difficulty: ✵ ✵ = Moderate

Topic: Assessment

Practice Behavior: Selecting appropriate intervention strategies

_____

_____

44. Foreclosures have risen, partly due to the declining economic condition of the economy. As a result, homelessness has increased and families are affected. Many in the community are unaware of the extent to which families are forced out of their homes. As a result, Stay Together Housing (STH), a community-based housing association, hires Edward, a social work housing advocate, to plan a campaign to secure governmental foreclosed homes for families displaced due to foreclosure. In this case, the first recommendation might be that:

a. Edward approach the town council and the mayor and ask for their support for rent control.

b. Edward focus on real estate interests and win their voluntary cooperation.

c. Edward develop a survey and problem analysis that describes the factors associated with the problem and publicize it throughout the community through communications such as email, word of mouth, and social network media.

d. Edward create a partnership with an assortment of organizations, including banks and federal agencies.

Difficulty: ✵ ✵ = Moderate

Topic: Intervention

Practice Behavior: Initiating actions to achieve organizational goals

_____

_____

45. Leah is a second year MSW intern placed at a substance abuse treatment center. In establishing a professional relationship with one of her clients, Franklin, the first action is that:

   a. Leah must display a certain degree of healthy skepticism toward Franklin.
   b. Leah must first communicate positive acceptance toward Franklin.
   c. Leah must first convey a sense of objective observation toward Franklin.
   d. Leah must communicate a neutral attitude toward Franklin.

   Difficulty: ✲ = Easy
   Topic: Engagement
   Practice Behavior: Using empathy and other interpersonal skills

   _____

   _____

46. Carolyn, a MSW student, is interning at the Community Services Board in a small mid-western town and notices her next door neighbor, Greg, in the waiting room of the agency. The most appropriate action to take is for:

   a. Carolyn to greet her neighbor Greg and ask whom he is there to see.
   b. Carolyn to greet her neighbor Greg and introduce him to other staff members who may still be at the agency.
   c. Carolyn to greet her neighbor Greg without engaging in conversation.
   d. Carolyn to ignore Greg's presence and say nothing to him.

   Difficulty: ✲ = Easy
   Topic: Engagement
   Practice Behavior: Preparing for action with individuals, families, groups, organizations, and communities

   _____

   _____

47. Dawn, age nineteen, has been fighting an addiction to methamphetamine since age fifteen has learned that she is four weeks pregnant. At her interview with her social worker, Henry, she shared that the news of her pregnancy has motivated her to stop using meth and she expressed an interest to learn steps to take that would protect the health of her baby. The best interventions that will enhance the client's capacities is for:

   a. Henry to help Dawn enroll in a drug treatment program that emphasizes immediate and total withdrawal.

b. Henry to help Dawn understand that suddenly stopping meth might be dangerous for her health and that of her infant and that she should seek expert medical help to gradually detoxify.

   c. Henry to tell Dawn to wait until her pregnancy is over before attempting to do anything about her addiction.

   d. Henry to refer Dawn to resources that will provide her with the medical help needed to gradually detoxify, and assist her in applying for Medicaid, WIC, and any other programs she is eligible for.

Difficulty: ✿ ✿ = Moderate

Topic: Intervention

Practice Behavior: Implementing prevention interventions, enhancing client capacities

_____

_____

48. Skylar, a recent MSW graduate, is unit supervisor for an agency that provides counseling services to women and children infected with HIV/AIDS. In an effort to ensure that the most effective, well-trained, and experienced workers remain with the unit, the most effective actions are for:

   a. Skylar to develop more educational and in-service opportunities for health care professional staff to improve knowledge and skills regarding HIV/AIDS service delivery.

   b. Skylar to increase opportunities for new and more varied assignments.

   c. Skylar to increase worker satisfaction by providing each health care professional with positive feedback and involving them in policy, planning, and case decisions.

   d. Skylar to support higher salary increases and provide assurances of long-term employment to the current health care professionals.

Difficulty: ✿ ✿ = Moderate

Topic: Evaluation

Practice Behavior: Initiating actions to achieve organizational goals

_____

_____

49. Jacob, a recent LMSW, has just begun providing marital therapy to Barbara and David. During the initial interview, Jacob learns that David was hospitalized in the last year because of a suicide attempt due to chronic depression. In an effort to design an intervention, the best option is for:

   a. Jacob to assist with tangible issues that can ease the stresses both Barbara and David experience.

b. Jacob to refer both Barbara and David for individual treatment and Barbara to a support group.

   c. Jacob to help increase David's awareness of how his actions affect his wife, Barbara.

   d. Jacob to support the couple's relationship, help Barbara understand her husband, David, and provide opportunities for both Barbara and David to express their feelings.

Difficulty: ✸✸ = Moderate

Topic: Evaluation

Practice Behavior: Critically analyzing, monitoring, and evaluating interventions

_____

_____

50. Lily, age twenty-three, has been in and out of the child welfare system since she was age twelve. As an adult she has had three Department of Family and Children Services (DFCS) cases, two unsubstantiated and one substantiated. She is currently working her DFCS case plan and doing well. Lily was previously in an abusive and violent relationship with her three-year-old daughters' father, Donald, who also abused her child. Lily relies heavily on her mother, Doris, who buys her food, pays all of her bills, and takes her to and from the bus stop near her home. Lily has asked if she could continue her counsel with her social worker, Charles, although her case plan will be terminated and she will have full custody of her daughter. If Lily were to remain in treatment with Charles, her treatment plan would have to be updated. One goal of treatment in this case would be for:

   a. Charles, the social worker, to continue counseling the family until he is satisfied that Lily has worked through her dependence on others.

   b. Charles to bring Doris to treatment and help her understand that she is enabling her daughter Lily.

   c. Charles to help Lily assert her independence by helping her to understand the dynamics of her dependency on her mother.

   d. Charles, the social worker, to work with Lily on developing more independent patterns of behavior, such as finding employment, purchasing a car, and gradually moving toward self-reliance.

Difficulty: ✸✸✸ = Challenging

Topic: Intervention

Practice Behavior: Facilitating transitions and endings

_____

_____

51. As part of her behavioral treatment plan, Melody, a second year MSW intern, is practicing the technique of positive reinforcement as a strategy with her client Nora. The best steps to successfully analyze, monitor, and evaluate this strategy is for:

   a. Melody to avoid situations that trigger Nora's behaviors that need to be extinguished.
   b. Melody to offer encouragement when Nora fails at a task and knows she has failed.
   c. Melody to reward the target or desired behavior when Nora demonstrates it.
   d. Melody to criticize Nora when competence is not demonstrated.

   Difficulty: ✲✲ = Moderate

   Topic: Evaluation

   Practice Behavior: Critically analyzing, monitoring, and evaluating

_____

_____

52. William is the family social worker for the Karstens family. His main client, Greg Karstens, is a developmentally challenged thirty-one-year-old who has always lived with his parents, Timothy and Connie Karstens. Mr. and Mrs. Karstens report that Greg has become unmanageable and irritable and that he refuses to leave home for special programs designed for him. They further share with William that Greg is easily angered whenever his parents ask him to do anything. They are requesting help. The best recommendation for this case is for:

   a. William to continue counseling with Greg.
   b. William to refer Greg and his family to an agency that specializes in dysfunctional families of adult children.
   c. William to provide residential treatment to Greg, since he refuses to leave the house.
   d. William to work with Greg and his parents, Timothy and Connie, and together determine the best ways to help resolve their problems.

   Difficulty: ✲ = Easy

   Topic: Intervention

   Practice Behavior: Helping resolve client problems

_____

_____

53. Whitney, a second year MSW student intern, is facilitating a group as a school social worker. Sonny, one of the group members, stands up for Daniel, another group member, who is being bullied during the group session. Sonny sees his actions as heroic and unselfish, while the other

group members view his actions negatively. After some discussion in the group, Sonny is unwilling to hear the group's opinions. In this case the best action for the facilitator to take is for:

a. Whitney to allow the discussion to continue, since others in the group may help Sonny to see things differently.
b. Whitney to suggest the group role-play the incident in an effort to process it.
c. Whitney reflect her apparent unwillingness to resolve the matter.
d. Whitney to reflect that the issue seems to represent an unresolved conflict with authority.

Difficulty: ✵ ✵ = Moderate
Topic: Assessment
Practice Behavior: Selecting appropriate intervention strategies

---

54. Haley, a social work intern in her final semester of her MSW program, is leading a parenting group for families mandated by DFCS to receive parenting classes as part of their case plan. The two primary goals of the group are to (1) assist parents in improving their relationships with their children, and (2) learn coping skills in dealing effectively with their children's difficult behaviors. Haley will assist the group in learning behavioral techniques. The most useful strategy is for:

a. Haley to help the group develop short-term, time-limited group exercises that use case examples for teaching purposes.
b. Haley to assist with small group counseling sessions that train parents in the use of problem solving skills.
c. Haley to assist in the development of psycho-educational groups that use structured cognitive behavioral approaches.
d. Haley to support groups for parents to share issues and discover ways to deal with misbehavior.

Difficulty: ✵ ✵ = Moderate
Topic: Engagement
Practice Behavior: Preparing for action with individuals, families, groups, organizations, and communities

55. Megan, a second year MSW student, is struggling with her client Bob's guilt regarding a situation that she discussed with her agency supervisor. The best action in this situation is for:

   a. Megan to assist Bob in seeing that guilt is very unhealthy and help him find ways to rid himself of guilt.
   b. Megan to accept and understand Bob's guilt, and allow him to ventilate.
   c. Megan to help Bob understand what he has done.
   d. Megan to learn how to always relieve Bob's guilt.

   Difficulty: ✵ = Easy
   Topic: Engagement
   Practice Behavior: Preparing for action with individuals, families, groups, organizations, and communities

   _____

   _____

56. Albert, a social work intern, is working as a medical social worker at Leeford Hospital. He has been asked to lead a support group for individuals infected with HIV/AIDS. A challenge that Albert might encounter regarding the group is:

   a. Leeford Hospital's need to respond to public concerns and issues regarding adequate treatment of AIDS victims.
   b. The group members' need for information on new drugs and innovative treatment modalities.
   c. The members' feelings and experiences of isolation and their lack of support from family, friends, and the community.
   d. Leeford Hospital finding new ways to cope with issues related to liability and insurance claims.

   Difficulty: ✵= Easy
   Topic: Engagement
   Practice Behavior: Preparing for action with individuals, families, groups, organizations, and communities

   _____

   _____

57. Mathis is in his last semester of his second year in an MSW program and interning at Families Now, an agency that provides individual and marital counseling to families who served in the armed forces. In setting service goals with clients Mary and Harry, it is most important that:

   a. Mathis, the social worker, allows most of the service goal setting to come from Mary and Harry.
   b. Most of the service goals should come from Mathis, the social worker.
   c. The goal setting process should be a collaborative process between Mary and Harry and Mathis.
   d. The service goal setting should be done early in the interviewing process by Mathis.

   Difficulty: ✵ = Easy
   Topic: Intervention
   Practice Behavior: Preparing for action with individuals, families, groups, organizations, and communities

   _____

   _____

58. Larry, an LCSW, is director of Positive Association, a social service agency that mentors single custodian fathers. As Positive Association's program develops and its staff grows, Larry is likely to be concerned about:

   a. Envisioning the results for his staff at Positive Associations.
   b. Providing support services for Positive Associations staff.
   c. Developing a formal structure for Positive Associations.
   d. Developing leadership for Positive Associations.

   Difficulty: ✵ = Easy
   Topic: Intervention
   Practice Behavior: Initiating actions to achieve organizational goals

   _____

   _____

59. James, an advanced year MSW student, is interning at a social service agency that addresses the educational and medical needs of gay teens. As part of the agency's outreach, James communicates with community centers, social media networks, and other community groups to locate gay teens and inform them of possible services available to them. Of particular importance to individual workers engaged in this activity is their:

   a. Ability to adapt community organizational skills to social action.

b. Need to be positive about gay teens and mindful of homophobic influences on themselves and others.
   c. Knowledge and understanding of the agency's program philosophy, its policies, and its relationships with other agencies.
   d. Ability to maintain a clearly defined contract consistent with agency sponsorship.

Difficulty: ⭐ = Easy
Topic: Interventions
Practice Behavior: Negotiating, mediating, and advocating for clients

_____

_____

60. Peter, a recent MSW graduate, is concerned about properly engaging professionally with his clients. He has placed particular emphasis on Jamie, one of his female clients, who has boundary emphasis. In this particular relationship:

   a. Peter should be concerned about a counter-transference reaction from Jamie.
   b. Peter should be concerned about Jamie's desire to change the original contract and add new goals.
   c. Peter should be concerned about the worker–client relationship.
   d. Peter should be concerned about transference reaction.

Difficulty: ⭐ = Easy
Topic: Intervention
Practice Behavior: Implementing prevention interventions and enhancing client capacities

_____

_____

61. After college, Phillip is unable to secure employment, so he goes back to live with his mother, Samantha, and her boyfriend, Darren, claiming that he cannot afford an apartment and, as Samantha's son, he has a right not be homeless and live with them. However, Phillip constantly argues with his mother, disrespects her, and places inappropriate demands on their relationship. He gives the impression that he has not separated from his mother. As the family social worker, you would first:

   a. Conduct a session with Phillip's mother, Samantha.
   b. Work with his mother's boyfriend, Darren.
   c. Conduct an individual session solely with Phillip.

d. Work with his mother, Samantha, and her boyfriend, Darren.

Difficulty: ✳ = Easy
Topic: Intervention
Practice Behavior: Implementing prevention interventions, enhancing client capacities

_____

_____

62. Phillip is very resistant to your help. Possibly, because of his past sense of entitlement from his mother and his lack of relationship with his mother's boyfriend, Darren. As the family social worker, to diminish Phillip's resistance you:

   a. Would be firm with Phillip and insist on answers to all questions.
   b. Would remind Phillip of his reasons for seeking assistance and stress the importance of cooperation.
   c. Would increase Phillip's anxiety to increase his motivation.
   d. Would lead Phillip to acknowledge his hesitance about accepting help.

Difficulty: ✳ = Easy
Topic: Assessment
Practice Behavior: Assessing client strengths and limitations

_____

_____

63. Jose, a Licensed Master Social Worker (LMSW), organizes a group of families who are upset and annoyed about the care they receive at the local community services board. The families are demanding improved services that include Spanish-speaking, customer-friendly workers who are at least courteous in their service delivery. The group meets for several weeks and is now considering strategies to present in their demands to the director. The most effective initial strategy is for:

   a. Jose to arrange a sit-in at the community services board, since the director is likely to be unreceptive to the community and will most likely reject the demands.
   b. Jose prepares a list of demands to see the director, since the worker can relate on a peer level.
   c. Jose to contact the media and have them do a story on the staff's behavior.

d. Jose to arrange for the leaders of the group to meet with the director and present their demands, since they are the service recipients.

Difficulty: ✳✳ = Moderate
Topic: Assessment
Practice Behavior: Selecting appropriate intervention strategies

_____

_____

64. Marvin, a social work student interning as a school social worker at one of the local high schools, discusses problems of unexcused absences and disruptive behaviors with a group of teenage boys. The boys are from dysfunctional family situations that are mostly headed by females and have experienced a number of problems both in and out of school. At one of the group meetings, Alex's uncontrollable laughter and restless body movements irritate the group, however, he continues, conscious of the effect he is having. Several members ask Alex to stop, but he becomes argumentative and hostile. The group wants to eject him. Marvin, the social worker, would most likely:

a. Question the group about why they want to eject Alex but indicate as the facilitator of the group that it is his decision to determine who stays or leaves.
b. Discuss with the group their rationale for wanting Alex out of the group and use their irritation to move the discussion to the group's purpose.
c. Be protective of Alex and try to set a tone of tolerance for his unusual behavior.
d. Indicate to the group that their objections to Alex's behavior need to be more constructive and focused.

Difficulty: ✳✳✳ = Challenging
Topic: Engagement
Practice Behavior: Preparing for action with individuals, families, groups, organizations, and communities

_____

_____

Essay Questions

1. Discuss the engagement process with your clients in relation to the acronym APSWE and provide an example.

2. By what means would you go about facilitating APSWE in your field agency with the client to whom you least like to provide service delivery?

3. In preparing for action with your client base, what are some of the various identities as a social work clinician, as well as the diversity of roles and responsibilities toward your client base, that you have experienced?

4. Discuss your understanding of the role of an educator when preparing for actions with individuals, families, groups, and communities.

5. Discuss what you know to be "good interpersonal skills" and what they enable you to do as an advanced or second year MSW student practitioner.

6. Discuss the concepts of Piaget's intellectual development theory and how it aids in developing a mutually agreed-on focus of work and outcomes for your client base.

7. By what means would you go about facilitating APSWE in your field agency with a court mandated client whom you feel least prefers to utilize your services?

8. Identify the assessment relative to your recognizing the knowledge and skill set needed to practice professional social work.

9. Discuss the assessment process of the crisis intervention-based approach.

10. Identify and discuss at least one of Cowger's practice guidelines that foster a strengths perspective when assessing client strengths.

11. Identify and discuss no less than two of the methods by which to collected or gather information on your clients.

12. Discuss the by-product of utilizing the interpersonal skill of empathy regarding your client base and provide at least two examples of how you have effectively used it, as well as inappropriately utilized it, with a client.

13. Discuss the assessment process of the psychodynamic theory-based approach.

14. Discuss two of the three fundamental components of the integrated service delivery model when developing mutually agreed-on intervention goals and objectives for your clients.

15. What are some areas to consider when selecting appropriate intervention strategies for your clients?

16. Identify and discuss the various settings that allow you to initiate actions that result in the achievement of organizational goals.

17. Discuss the system that you must have in place when assessing client behaviors.

18. What are primary, secondary, and tertiary preventions, and how do they enhance client capacities to implement prevention interventions?

19. What does it mean, as an advanced or second year Master Social Work student, to help resolve client problems?

20. Discuss what negotiating for clients entails as an advanced or second year MSW student practitioner and provide an example of how you have demonstrated it in the field or witnessed it demonstrated.

21. What does it mean to critically analyze, monitor, and evaluate interventions on behalf of your client?

22. Discuss what advocating for the client entails as an advanced or second year MSW student practitioner and provide an example how you have demonstrated it in the field or witnessed it demonstrated.

23. Discuss the importance of assessing client limitations when designing an intervention.

24. Discuss what it means to facilitate transitions and endings as an MSW student practitioner.

25. Discuss some of the commonly known errors to avoid when critically analyzing, monitoring, and evaluating interventions on behalf of your client.

26. Discuss what mediating for the client entails as an advanced or second year MSW student practitioner and provide an example of how you have demonstrated it in the field or witnessed it demonstrated.

Role-Play Exercise: Will Mary K Keep Avon?

Actions and responses to the role-play "Will Mary K Keep Avon?" will vary and depend on your individual characteristics, personal experience, and professional knowledge and are from your own perspective. Learn and enjoy!

You are an advanced or second year social worker student working with a Mary K and her daughter Avon, who are receiving therapy because Mary K is in the midst an ugly divorce. Mary K's attorney asks you to write a letter to support Mary K's custody of Avon. You are placed in an uncomfortable position, because you have never seen the father.

In seeking resolution to these issues, role-play several different scenarios that might depict how you would (1) engage, (2) assess, (3) intervene, and (4) evaluate this situation. Participants must role-play how they would go about using evidence-based research to inform practice and experience to inform scientific inquiry.

Practice with MySocialWorkLab

Visit **MySocialWorkLab** at www.mysocialworklab.com to watch these competency-based videos.

Watch

Engagement, Assessment, Intervention, Evaluation—**Engagement**

Engagement, Assessment, Intervention, Evaluation—**Assessment**

Engagement, Assessment, Intervention, Evaluation—**Intervention**

Engagement, Assessment, Intervention, Evaluation—**Evaluation**

References

Brown, R. E., Reed, C. S, Bates, L. V., Knaggs, D., Casey, K. M., & Barnes, J. V. (2006). The transformative engagement process: Foundations and supports for university–community partnerships. *Journal of Higher Education Outreach and Engagement, 11*(1), 9.

Cowger, C. (1994). Assessing client strengths: Clinical assessment for client empowerment. *Journal of Social Work, 39*(3), 262–268.

Fetterman, D. (2005). A window into the heart and soul of empowerment evaluation: Looking through the lens of empowerment evaluation principles. In D. Fetterman and A. Wandersman (Eds.), *Empowerment evaluation principles in practice.* New York: Guilford Press.

Gambrill, E., & Gibbs, L. (2009). *Critical thinking for helping professionals: A skills-based workbook* (3rd Ed.). New York: Oxford University Press.

Patton, M. Q. (1997). *Utilization-focused evaluation* (3rd Ed.). Thousand Oaks, CA: Sage.

Patton, M. Q. (2007). Process use as a usefulism. In J. B. Cousins (Ed.), *Process use in theory, research and practice. New directions for evaluation, no. 116,* 99–112. San Francisco, CA: Wiley.

Rogers, A. T. (2006). *Human behavior in the social environment.* New York: McGraw-Hill.

Schriver, J. M. (2011). *Human behavior and the social environment: Shifting paradigms in essential knowledge for social work practice* (5th Ed.). Boston: Pearson Education/ Allyn & Bacon.

Weiss, C. H. (1998). Have we learned anything new about the use of evaluation? *American Journal of Evaluation, 19,* 21–33.

Below find some of the answers to the multiple choice questions in this Workbook.

CHAPTER 1

1.	b	**11.**	C	**21.**	d
3.	b	**13.**	b	**23.**	b
5.	c	**15.**	c	**25.**	d
7.	b	**17.**	a	**27.**	c
9.	b	**19.**	b	**29.**	c

CHAPTER 2

1.	C	**9.**	b	**17.**	b
3.	b	**11.**	c	**19.**	a
5.	c	**13.**	c		
7.	b	**15.**	b		

CHAPTER 3

1.	d	**7.**	a	**13.**	c
3.	d	**9.**	d	**15.**	a
5.	c	**11.**	a		

CHAPTER 4

1.	a	**9.**	c	**17.**	d
3.	d	**11.**	c	**19.**	d
5.	d	**13.**	c		
7.	a	**15.**	a		

CHAPTER 5

1. c	7. d	13. a
3. c	9. b	15. c
5. c	11. b	

CHAPTER 6

1. c	5. b	9. a
3. d	7. a	

CHAPTER 7

1. c	5. a	9. b
3. b	7. c	

CHAPTER 8

1. b	5. d	9. d
3. c	7. c	

CHAPTER 9

1. b	5. c	9. b
3. c	7. d	

CHAPTER 10

1. c	23. b	45. b
3. d	25. b	47. d
5. c	27. c	49. d
7. d	29. d	51. b
9. c	31. b	53. b
11. b	33. a	55. b
13. b	35. d	57. c
15. b	37. a	59. b
17. a	39. b	61. c
19. d	41. c	63. d
21. c	43. a	